"IN TE DOMINE SPERAMUS"

Essays
on
Rhode Island
Military History

Robert Grandchamp

HERITAGE BOOKS
2018

HERITAGE BOOKS

AN IMPRINT OF HERITAGE BOOKS, INC.

Books, CDs, and more—Worldwide

For our listing of thousands of titles see our website
at
www.HeritageBooks.com

Published 2018 by
HERITAGE BOOKS, INC.
Publishing Division
5810 Ruatan Street
Berwyn Heights, Md. 20740

Heritage Books by the author:

From Providence to Fort Hell: Letters from Company K, Seventh Rhode Island Volunteers
"In Te Domine Speramus:" Essays on Rhode Island Military History
*"Now Show Them What Rhode Island Can Do!": An Annotated
Bibliography of Rhode Island Civil War Sources*
"We Lost Many Brave Men": A Statistical History of the Seventh Rhode Island Volunteers
"With their usual ardor": Scituate, Rhode Island and the American Revolution

International Standard Book Number
Paperbound: 978-0-7884-5830-9

"Speak to the Past and it Shall Teach Thee"

-Wilberforce Eames

iv

For my Grandfather

CONTENTS

Introduction

In life we often find a calling. Something that we are profoundly passionate about that becomes our life's work. I found my calling in the winter of 2001. Raised in a family that frequently traveled to Pennsylvania for summer vacations, which always included a stop at Gettysburg, I had long had an interest in the Civil War, reading classics such as Bruce Catton, *Voices from the Civil War*, Bill Marvel's writings, and others. Two events changed my life in 2001 that made Civil War history my calling.

One day in early January 2001, while helping my grandmother clean out her attic, we discovered an old, rusty World War II ammunition chest that was filled with family papers. My grandmother's maiden name was Knight. Growing up she had taken me to visit scenes of her family's past, visiting graveyards, and driving around the town of Scituate, where the family originated. The Knights were among the earliest settlers of western Rhode Island, and included a *Mayflower* connection through the Rogers family. They had lived for over two hundred years in Scituate before being forced to relocate to Coventry and Warwick after the Scituate Reservoir was built. My grandmother was fond to say that the Knights were "planted here" in the rocky soil of western Rhode Island.

While looking at family documents in the box, we found pictures of my great-grandfather, a former assistant postmaster in West Warwick, Rhode Island, in addition to some documents about my grandfather's lace mill he once ran. One small item piqued my interest. It was a battered, old book with crumbling pages, underlined in many places, with a cracked binding. The book was titled *Genealogy of the Potter Family*; one of many families such as the Colvins, Potters, Fields, Fiskes, and Mattesons that had married into the Knight family. Laid into the book was a poem titled "Lines on the Death of Alfred S. Knight" I was intrigued; the poem was about a relative that died in the Civil War.

Using the genealogy book, I discovered that Knight had served as a member of Company C of the Seventh Rhode Island Volunteers and died of pneumonia on January 31, 1863 while serving in the army. I knew I had to find out more about my Civil War relative. We soon traveled to Scituate, where we conducted research in the town hall archives, gathering more information on the Knight family. In addition, we visited Alfred's grave on the Scituate Reservoir property . A chance encounter later that year led to the discovery of Alfred's letters in Scituate. Soon, I had a binder of material on my uncle. It would not be until 2011, that I would finally obtain a photograph of him, finally getting to see the face of the man who had fueled my passion. While I gathered much material on my uncle and his service, I also became interested in the Seventh Rhode Island Volunteers as a whole. I wanted to learn more about the regiment that he served in.

The second event of 2001 was the publication of the book *My Brave Boys: To War with Colonel Cross and the Fighting Fifth* written by Mike Pride and Mark Travis. My grandparents had long had a summer cottage on Lake Winnipesaukee in Meredith, New Hampshire. Here I spent every summer until I was nineteen, fishing, boating, and traveling around the Granite State. It was and remains a very special place for me. I discovered the book and convinced my mother to buy me a copy. I devoured the book, reading it again and again. The story of the Fifth New Hampshire was an amazing one, a regiment that lost more men in combat than any other Union infantry unit. I was especially intrigued by the colonel of the Fifth, Edward E. Cross. What made *My Brave Boys* have an impact on my life was that previous to this, I had only thought of the Civil War as an event taking place on the battlefields of Virginia, Pennsylvania, and elsewhere in the South. The authors brought the experience of the battlefield back home to New Hampshire. In the pages of *My Brave Boys,* I could read how the events that occurred at Antietam, Chancellorsville, Gettysburg, and elsewhere had a profound impact on the communities in New Hampshire such as Concord, Lebanon, Portsmouth, and

Claremont, all places I had visited in my youth. In my later years I became friends with author Mike Pride who assisted me in the writing of my biography of Colonel Cross.

After reading *My Brave Boys,* I was determined to find similar stories in Rhode Island. It soon became apparent that Rhode Island had a vast literature of Civil War books to be read. I soon began to purchase and enjoy regimental histories, as well as published letters and diaries written by Rhode Islanders. I made frequent trips to libraries, cemeteries, and archives around Rhode Island, gathering copies of material. One day while visiting an antique store in Richmond, Rhode Island, I discovered a letter written by Peleg E. Peckham. From my research on the Seventh Rhode Island, I knew he had served as a captain in the regiment and was killed in the closing days of the war. I begged my grandmother to purchase the letter for me; at fifteen dollars, she could not understand why someone would pay so much for an old piece of paper. She bought me the letter, the first of many I would later add to my collection. For my collecting, I was awarded the 2007 Margaret B. Stillwell Prize from the John Russell Bartlett Society at Brown University. I am still proud to state I am the only Rhode Island College graduate to be given this honor.

While I started collecting material and reading all that could be read on the Civil War, I discovered, in 2002, that there was a very active Civil War community in Rhode Island. I first joined the Rhode Island Civil War Round Table, a scholarly group that met in Cranston each month listening to lectures on the Civil War. I became good friends with Mark Dunkelman, whose own lifetime work on the 154th New York Infantry later became the model I would follow for my own study of the Seventh Rhode Island. I also joined the Sons of Union Veterans of the Civil War in Smithfield. I was happy to become a member of Colonel Zenas R. Bliss Camp 12, named after the man who had commanded the Seventh Rhode Island during the war. As a member of Bliss Camp, I helped flag Civil War veteran's graves in western Rhode Island for Memorial Day, assisted in replacing headstones of Civil War veterans, and took part in other events. I also joined a local reenacting group, Battery B, First Rhode Island Light Artillery.

Instead of just reading about the Civil War, I began to live it, traveling around the country, spending my weekends in authentic reproduction uniforms, living the life of a Union soldier. All of these groups were a great way to expand my passion and knowledge of Civil War history. It also was how I spent my high school years.

I graduated from high school in 2004 and knew that I wanted to study history. I went to Rhode Island College; it was inexpensive at the time, close to home, and had a good history program. Also, being in Providence, Rhode Island College provided me with a base from which I could make trips between classes to the wonderful repositories at Brown University, the John Carter Brown Library, Rhode Island State Archives, Rhode Island Historical Society, and the Providence Public Library. Providence is a wonderful city to work as a historian in. Working under the direction of several professors, including Dr. J. Stanley Lemons, who imparted a wealth of knowledge in me, I learned much during my six years at Rhode Island College. In 2010, I graduated with a Master of Arts degree in American history. My master's thesis was a biographical study and compilation of the letters of George Lee Gaskell. A remarkable soldier from Sterling, Connecticut, Gaskell was highly educated and spoke several languages. He served in Battery G, First Rhode Island Light Artillery, as well as the Fourteenth Rhode Island Heavy Artillery. After the Civil War Gaskell remained in Louisiana, was involved in Reconstruction, and became an advocate for black rights. To complete my research on Gaskell, I later made a very long drive to Cincinnati, Ohio to visit his final resting place. My thesis was later published in 2015 by Pelican Publishing as *A Connecticut Yankee at War: The Life and Letters of George Lee Gaskell.*

My college years were spent largely researching and writing about the Civil War, volunteering in several local museums, and reenacting the Civil War. I volunteered at the Paine House Museum of the Western Rhode Island Civic Historical Society in Coventry and at the Pettaquamscutt Historical Society in South Kingstown, learning the ins and outs of working at a museum. Reenacting also took up a large amount of my time. I

4

also had what I considered the coolest summer job one could find. From 2007-2010, I served as a National Park Ranger, spending my summers working at Harpers Ferry National Park and Shenandoah National Park. Wearing Civil War uniforms or the famed Smokey Bear Ranger Hat, I gave tours, conducted research, and staffed an information desk. It was some of the best years of my life, as I lived and worked where the history I loved took place. Living in Harpers Ferry, I could be at Antietam in twenty minutes, or Gettysburg in an hour. It was truly one of the best experiences I ever had; in all I spent over a year living in the Shenandoah Valley, away from Rhode Island for the first time.

For a time, I wanted to be a National Park Ranger more than anything else. Unfortunately for many young historians, becoming a full time Ranger is the equivalent of becoming a NASA astronaut; it is nearly impossible to get a full-time job. I eventually found work with another Federal agency, but never forgot my Ranger years. In 2012, I was invited to lead a program called Rhode Island Day at Antietam National Battlefield which was well attended by Rhode Islanders and others. Mostly however, in my spare time, I wrote history.

When I was sixteen, after reading hundreds and hundreds of history books, I decided to try my hand at writing. My first book was *With their usual ardor: Scituate, Rhode Island and the American Revolution,* which was followed by *With High and Holy Aim: Alfred Sheldon Knight and the Civil War,* both of which, in retrospect, I look at as poor, amateurish works. However, they were good training opportunities to learn the historian's craft. I followed up these books with *Providence to Fort Hell: Letters from Company K, Seventh Rhode Island Volunteers,* which is a compilation of edited and transcribed letters written by men from one company of the Seventh. This book prepared me for researching and writing *The Seventh Rhode Island Infantry in the Civil War.* Published in 2008, this book was my first professional work. Deeply researched from primary sources, and highly illustrated, it told the full story of the Seventh Rhode Island. The book opened up many doors for me. I began to review Civil War books for a variety of publications and also embarked on a lecture

5

tour of Rhode Island. I followed up a year later in 2009 with *The Boys of Adams' Battery G: The Civil War through the eyes of a Union light artillery unit.* A regimental history of Battery G, First Rhode Island Light Artillery, I consider this book to be my best, telling the full story of this unit which never had a history written before it.

My 2008 publication of *The Seventh Rhode Island Infantry* opened up the door to my greatest endeavor. In 2006, I made contact with retired Brigadier General Richard Valente for a tour of the Benefit Street Arsenal in Providence. The arsenal was the mustering point for all the men who served in the First Rhode Island Light Artillery and is now a military museum. General Valente gave me a fantastic tour and we exchanged contact info. One June night in 2008, while I was eating dinner with some friends in Winchester, Virginia, near the site where several Rhode Island units had fought in the autumn of 1864, he called me out of the blue with a proposal that I instantly accepted.

Several years earlier, the Providence Marine Corps of Artillery, a veterans group composed of retired members of the 103rd Field Artillery of the Rhode Island National Guard, had begun to research and write a bicentennial history of the unit. An outline was made, but little progress had been made on the book. General Valente asked me to finish the project. For the next two years, I worked nearly full time on the project, gathering research, interviewing veterans, finding photographs, and putting the project together. When it was published in 2011 as *Rhody Redlegs,* the book was widely regarded by both military and civilians as a model unit history. For my role in the project, I was awarded the Order of St. Barbara by the Rhode Island National Guard, becoming the first civilian recipient of the highest honor given out by the field artillery community. In 2015, I returned to the Benefit Street Arsenal to assist in the dedication of a plaque to honor the seven members of Battery G, First Rhode Island Light Artillery who had earned the Medal of Honor for their actions on April 2, 1865 at Petersburg, Virginia.

In 2011, unable to find any employment in my beloved Rhode Island, I moved away, to the hills of rural Vermont to work for the government. Eventually I would buy and restore an old farmhouse in a quiet village, and marry a wonderful woman, who like me grew up in Warwick, Rhode Island and went to Rhode Island College before moving to Vermont. While I no longer reside in the Ocean State, my home is a museum to the place of my birth and heritage. A large anchor adorns our wall; jonny cake mix and Buddy Cianci pasta sauce are in our cupboard, while books on Rhode Island history and Civil War artifacts fill bookshelves. I am proud to state; I am a twelfth generation Rhode Islander and a first-generation Vermonter.

In the pages that follow is a compilation of essays I have written over the years regarding the military history of Rhode Island. Although small in size, Rhode Island history is big in significance. Since the American Revolution, and especially in the Civil War, Rhode Islanders have long contributed to the nation's defense. These essays, each different in its scope provide an overview into the Rhode Island military experience. Rhode Island's motto is Hope, originally styled as "In Te Domine Speramus," meaning "Our Hope is in Thee, Lord." Rhode Islanders have long used the anchor as a symbol of Hope, while wearing badges and buttons inscribed with the motto on their uniforms in times of conflict, or even now by the Rhode Island State Police and Rhode Island National Guard. It is my earnest Hope that these essays are both enjoyable and informative, while providing my fellow Rhode Islanders with a better understanding of the rich military heritage of the smallest state.

Robert Grandchamp
Jericho Center, Vermont

Chapter One:

"We landed beat them from fence to fence:"

The Battles of Prudence Island

The American Revolution was fought from Maine to Illinois, hundreds of military encounters occurring in what eventually became the United States of America. Among those events were two skirmishes on Prudence Island, a large island in Narragansett Bay in Rhode Island on January 12 and January 13, 1776. Although small events that did not alter the course of the war, the battles showed the mettle of the Rhode Island Militia and challenged British strategy in the Rhode Island theatre of operations.

The smallest colony, Rhode Island, with a population of 60,000, quickly responded to the events of Lexington and Concord, sending a brigade of three regiments and some artillery under Nathanael Greene to Boston that were eventually incorporated into the Continental Line.[1] From the beginning of the war however, Rhode Island's leaders were worried about the unique geography and the problems it posed to defending such a vast amount of coastline:

> Unfortunately for the inhabitants, this colony is scarcely any thing but a line of sea coast. From Providence to Point Judith; and from thence, to the Pawcatuck river is nearly eighty miles; on the east side of the bay, from Providence to Seaconnet Point, and including the east side of Seaconnet, until it meets the Massachusetts line is about

---

[1] Anthony Walker, *So Few the Brave: Rhode Island Continentals, 1775-1783.* (Newport: Seafield Press, 1981), 1-5.

9

fifty miles; besides which are the navigable rivers of Pawcatuck and Warren. On the west side of the colony doth not extend twenty miles; and on the east side, not more than eight miles from the sea coast above described. In the colony are also included several islands, all which are cultivated and fertile, and contribute largely to the public expense; the greater part of the above mentioned shores, are accessible to ships of war.[2]

Little did Rhode Island's political leaders know, but their colony would soon become a battle ground, and the islands in Narragansett Bay would play an important role in the Revolution.

With many of Rhode Island's men serving in the army besieging the British in Boston, an active call out went out to the various militia companies throughout the state to begin garrisoning strategic points along Narragansett Bay. Tasked with erecting batteries and other fortifications, the militia also erected a series of alert beacons that could be seen for miles to alert other companies to respond. Volunteering for varying terms of service, the militia provided invaluable service monitoring Narragansett Bay to ensure that British raiding parties did not attack settlements along the bay. This service would continue throughout the Revolution.[3]

Among the many Rhode Islanders suddenly caught up in the Revolution was thirty-five-year-old Captain Joseph Knight of Scituate. A well-off farmer, who owned large tracts of land, Knight was also involved in the Hope Furnace Company, managed by the Brown family of Providence that cast cannon for the Patriot cause. "He seems to have had a taste early for military life," and received his first commission as an ensign in 1766. Knight had steadily risen in rank to captain in 1774, taking command of the First Company of the Third Battalion of the Providence County

---

[2] John Russell Bartlett, ed. *Records of the Colony of Rhode Island and Providence Plantations: Volume VII.* (Providence: A. Crawford Greene, 1862), 424-426.

[3] For the most comprehensive view of this service refer to Edward Field, *Revolutionary Defenses in Rhode Island.* (Providence: Preston and Rounds, 1896)

Regiment. Throughout the winter of 1774-1775, Knight, like many knew that war was coming and trained his men frequently. Scituate, a large, rural farming town some distance from Narragansett Bay in western Rhode Island was thoroughly on the side of the American rebels.

Upon hearing of the Lexington Alarm on April 19, 1775, Knight called his men together and mustered the following morning. With fifty-two men he began his march to Boston, among the first Rhode Islanders to answer the call. After crossing into Massachusetts, the Scituate company received word that the British had returned to Boston, and Knight and his men returned to Scituate. With the American Revolution now underway, Captain Knight left his five children and wife Elizabeth at home in Scituate and proceeded to Warwick Neck on the western shores of Narragansett Bay, just below Providence. Situated mid-way up Narragansett Bay, the Neck would be garrisoned by Knight and his Scituate men for most of the Revolution.[4]

With the British garrison besieged in Boston by thousands of Americans under George Washington, supplies for the Crown forces became a focal point. Enjoying free access to the sea, without an effective American naval presence, Vice Admiral Richard Graves began to send ships of his fleet out of Boston to forage for supplies and raid coastal settlements. One squadron, under Captain James Wallace was dispatched to Narragansett Bay. Wallace, the commander of *H.M.S. Rose* had been in Rhode Island waters before, patrolling the entrance to Narragansett Bay since late 1774 to prevent smuggling operations.[5]

---

[4] C. C. Beaman, *An History Address, delivered in Scituate, R.I. July 4, 1876.* (Phenix, RI: Capron and Campbell, 1877), 41-43. John Russell Bartlett, *Census of the Inhabitants of the Colony of Rhode Island and Providence Plantations, 1774.* (Providence: Knowles, Anthony, & Co., 1858), 120. Joel A. Cohen, "Lexington and Concord: Rhode Island Reacts," *Rhode Island History,* Vol. 26, No. 4 (October 1967), 97-102. Joseph Knight Papers, Robert Grandchamp collection.
[5] W.G. Roelker, "The Patrol of Narragansett Bay (1774-76) by H.M.S. Rose, Captain James Wallace," *Rhode Island History,* Vol. 7, No. 1 (January 1948), 12-19.

Captain Wallace became the scourge of Narragansett Bay as he kept most shipping in port, demanded supplies from Newport and neighboring communities, and threatened to bombard Newport if his demands were not met. Also operating in Narragansett Bay alongside *H.M.S. Rose* was *H.M.S. Glasgow* and *H.M.S. Swan*. While Newport, a Loyalist stronghold provided Wallace with many supplies such as beef, rum, and dried peas that he sent on to General Thomas Gage's, there was not enough supplies to feed the British in Boston, as well as preventing the people of Newport from starving. With his supply line in Newport beginning to falter, Wallace began to look elsewhere in Narragansett Bay for supplies. The Rhode Island General Assembly knew Wallace could strike anywhere along the Narragansett Bay and ordered out additional militia companies to guard the coast. Captain Wallace attention soon turned to another large island, further up the bay. Up to this point, Rhode Islanders had freely given in to Captain Wallace's demands for supplies. This time, they would respond with blood.[6]

Situated at the midpoint of Narragansett Bay, Prudence Island is the third largest island in the bay. Part of the town of Portsmouth, Prudence is roughly six miles long, and one mile wide at it's widest. The island is situated one and a half miles south of Bristol, and the same distance from Warwick Neck. A farming community, largely raising potatoes and sheep, Prudence was home to thirty-three families and 228 people according to the 1774 Rhode Island census. With Captain Wallace and his squadron a continued threat to the people of Rhode Island, the General Assembly, not wanting Wallace to gain more supplies, ordered all livestock that could be moved off of Prudence, Patience, and Conanicut Islands to be moved onto the mainland to prevent it from falling into British hands. Unlike the majority of Newport residents, the people of Prudence were eager to join the "patriotic

---

[6] W.G. Roelker, "The Patrol of Narragansett Bay (1774-76) by H.M.S. Rose, Captain James Wallace," *Rhode Island History,* Vol. 9, No. 1 (January 1950), 11-22. William Bell Clark, ed. *Naval Documents of the American Revolution: Volume 4.* (Washington, D.C.: United States Navy, 1969), 48-51.

opposition to that system of tyranny and despotism designed for enslaving the American colonies." Likewise, the men of Prudence were "ready to contribute all reasonable assistance, towards prosecuting the present war, justly undertaken in defence of the United American colonies."[7]

Wallace and his men had visited Prudence briefly twice previously, the first time on August 24, 1775. Landing about 100 men on the island, they "plundered" the farm of John Allin, seizing some twenty sheep, thirty turkeys, bushels of corn, as well as a ton of hay. The supplies were taken onboard *H.M.S. Swan* and later sent to Boston. On November 17, 1775 Wallace's men pillaged two houses, taking, among other items, numerous articles of clothing, kettles, geese, and for unknown reasons "one large mahogany desk." While largely unopposed previously, Rhode Island had begun sending privateers out of Providence with an aim to attacking British shipping; occasionally these ships engaged in long range cannon duels with Wallace, with little damage to either side. For the most part, Wallace's mission in Narragansett Bay was largely successful. He purchased the majority of his supplies, resorting to raiding only when necessary.

Throughout 1775, these raids had largely been bloodless; several men were wounded on a raid near Stonington, Connecticut, while on December 10, 1775 a party of British Marines engaged in a brief skirmish on Conanicut Island, opposite Newport. The Rhode Island militiamen "had been enlisted but a few days, and arrived there but the evening before, in miserable condition." Despite the harsh New England winter weather, the militia stood up to the Marines in a brief skirmish, wounding nine of Wallace's men for one American casualty. Captain Wallace did

---

[7] Charles G. Maytum, "Early Prudence Island," 2: 68-73, typescript at East Greenwich Public Library, East Greenwich, Rhode Island. W.G. Roelker, "The Patrol of Narragansett Bay (1774-76) by H.M.S. Rose, Captain James Wallace," *Rhode Island History,* Vol. 9, No. 2 (April 1950), 52-58.

not learn from these events and instead decided to launch another raid on Prudence Island.[8]

Although he had been stripped of power by the General Assembly, Governor Joseph Wanton, a fervent Loyalist, continued to officially serve as the governor of Rhode Island, although he was soon to be deposed and replaced by Nicholas Cooke. On January 11, 1776, Wanton sent a letter to Captain Samuel Pearce, the commander of the Second Portsmouth Company, composed of men from Prudence Island that Captain Wallace would stop at Prudence on January 12 to purchase supplies. Wanton advised Pearce to comply with Wallace's demands and sell whatever livestock and provisions that remained on the island. The governor's letter sent Pearce into a rage. He immediately sent a reply letter back to Newport, telling Wanton "that whatever Wallace took off this island, would be taken off at the point of the bayonet." The die was now cast.[9]

It was clear to the inhabitants of Prudence that their island would soon become a battle ground. As the captain of the local militia company, Pearce ordered all women and children off the island. Bidding farewell to their wives and children, many of Pearce's men gave up their blankets to protect them from the winter cold as they rowed away to the safety of Bristol and Warwick. Taking with them as many household valuables and as much of the livestock that remained, it was a tearful scene, as the women realized that their husbands, fathers, brothers, and sons were about to engage in battle. Described as a "bitter cold winter day," January 11, 1776 would be the last time that many would

[8] Maytum, "Early Prudence," 72. Roelker, "Patrol of Narragansett Bay," (April 1950), 52-53. James Wallace to "Inhabitants of Newport," January 19, 1776, Rhode Island State Archives, Providence, RI. *Newport Mercury,* November 27, 1775.
[9] Cohen, "Lexington and Concord: Rhode Island Responds," 101-102. "Maytum, "Early Prudence," 76-77.

ever step foot on Prudence, settling instead on the mainland of Rhode Island.[10]

With the women and children off the island, all that remained were the men of Captain Pearce's Second Company composed of thirty-two men, among them were eleven African-American slaves who had been given weapons and instruction on how to use them. As was typical of a small island community, most of these men were related to each other; indeed, half of Pearce's company was composed of men from the Allin family. Dressed in their working clothes and armed with a variety of firearms, these citizen-soldiers prepared to fight to the most powerful nation on earth. Few had cartridge boxes, even fewer had bayonets. Captain Pearce knew that his thirty-two men could not make a determined stand against the British. Not knowing when or where the British would land, Pearce sent off hasty dispatches to Bristol and Warwick pleading for reinforcements.[11]

Colonel John Waterman commanded at Warwick Neck. His forces were comprised of several militia companies from neighboring towns, manning an earthwork containing two eighteen-pound cannon. Brigadier General William West, the commander of the Providence County Brigade was the overall commander of Patriot forces on the shores of Narragansett Bay and commanded from a post in Newport. In the early morning hours of January 12, 1776, General West sent out orders to a trusted subordinate, Captain Knight to take ten of his men and report immediately to Prudence on "fatigue duty." From their vantage point on Warwick Neck, Knight and his men had seen Wallace sailing along Narragansett Bay. It was clear with the civilians now off Prudence, that Knight and his twelve men as they

---

[10] Maytum, "Early Prudence," 73-77. Ezra Stiles, *The Literary Diary of Ezra Stiles: Volume I, January 1, 1769-March 13, 1776.* Edited by Franklin James Dexter. (New York: Charles Scribner's Sons, 1901), 653.
[11] Maytum, "Prudence Island," 77. Field, *Revolutionary Defenses,* 24-26. Beaman, *Scituate,* 45.

15

boarded the scow to take them the short distance across the Narragansett Bay that a fight was about to ensue.[12]

Also dispatched from Waterman's command was the Kentish Guards. A pre-war "independent company," composed of many of the elite from the West Bay towns of Coventry, Warwick, and East Greenwich. Among the members previously carried on the rolls was Nathanael Greene, James Mitchell Varnum, and Christopher Greene, now all serving in high office in the Continental Line. A cradle of colonial leadership, the Kentish Guards provided many of the officers who served in Rhode Island's Continental regiments. With new recruits and men who remained behind in East Greenwich, the Kentish Guards erected a fort to defend East Greenwich and like many of their neighbors spent their days manning it. The Guards would not make it into the fighting on January 12.[13]

From Bristol, Colonel William Richmond dispatched Ensign James Miller with a few men from Richmond's State Regiment. This was a large regiment of twelve companies that had been raised for full time state service to serve for one year in November 1775. While the terms of service of the militia varied from several days to a few months, the men of Richmond's Regiment and their brothers in Lippitt's Regiment were constantly on watch duty on the eastern shores of Narragansett Bay where most of the population and trade of Rhode Island occurred.[14]

At four o'clock in the afternoon of Friday, January 12, 1776 Captain Wallace anchored a half-mile off the south-east tip

---

[12] Field, *Revolutionary Defenses,* 82-84. Beaman, *Scituate,* 42. William West to Newport Town Council, January 30, 1776, Rhode Island State Archives. Rhode Island Militia Pay Receipts, Rhode Island State Archives.

[13] Daniel H. Greene, *History of the Town of East Greenwich and Adjacent Territory from 1677 to 1877.* (Providence: J.A. & R.A. Reid, 1877), 181-184.

[14] Walker, *So Few the Brave,* 11-22: 122-123. Catherine Williams, *Biography of Revolutionary Heroes.* (Providence: The Author, 1839), 303-305.

of Prudence Island, immediately opposite Dyer Island. Wallace landed about 250 British Marines and sailors on Prudence. The weather was freezing, daylight was fading, and there was a large amount of snow on the ground. Instantly, Wallace ordered six houses near his landing point put to the torch. Dr. Ezra Stiles, a Congregational minister and the librarian at the Redwood Library in Newport wrote, "I saw the flames from the Top of my house due North. He (Wallace) is now inhumanly spreading Barbarity, Desolation & Revenge there." As Stiles watched the flames on Prudence, he saw Patriot militia companies from Newport muster in the town and advance to garrison the fortifications around the harbor.[15]

The small force of militia and state troops, some fifty men all under the command of Captain Pearce moved up to engage the enemy. Ensign Miller ordered some men to set fire to a large quantity of hay that he believed the British wanted to capture. Although out of range, Pearce ordered his men to open fire. The American volley provoked a return in which a Private Williams of Richmond's Regiment was "shot through the breast, the ball passing directly under the breast bone, went in one side and came out the other." Williams was left where he fell and taken prisoner by the British; he was later released. The Americans returned fire "with much spirit."

It soon became clear to Knight and Pearce that the British force was much larger than they had expected. In the fighting one of Pearce's men went down instantly killed. After firing three volleys at the British, and determined to live to fight another day, the two captains ordered their men to retreat up the island, as they engaged in a running gun battle with the British up the island. In his official report, Captain Wallace wrote, "We landed beat them from fence to fence, for four miles into their country, firing and wasting the country as we advanced." In this engagement, another Prudence Island soldier was lost, captured by the British. Crown forces finally gained the upper hand and nearly surrounded the

[15] Stiles, *Literary Diary,* 653-654. William Bell Clark, ed. *Naval Documents of the American Revolution: Volume 3.* (Washington, D.C.: United States Navy, 1969), 800-801.

militia. Finally, with night falling, the Scituate and Portsmouth men, together with Ensign Miller "were obliged to make a precipitate retreat, and were taken off by their boats to Warwick Neck, the only thing which could have prevented their being hemmed in and cut to pieces." Captain Wallace acknowledged the loss of three men "slightly wounded." [16]

With American forces off the island, the British commenced burning homes, barns, and other structures on Prudence Island. The blaze lit up the night sky, being seen "for many a mile around." In Newport fear abounded that Wallace would return to destroy the town. Dr. Stiles called it, "A melancholly destressing prospect!" At 8:00 that night, "the People were fatigued with Cold, and fearing they might be Frost Bit." Wallace ordered his men back to their ships for the night. Many local militiamen saw the fire and flocked to Warwick Neck and Bristol, eager to exact revenge against the British. Unfortunately, there were few boats available to transport men to the island. As night combat was all but unknown in the eighteenth century, General West ordered his men to wait until morning to cross and engage the British again. [17]

After missing the fighting on January 12, Colonel Richard Fry, in the tradition of the New England Militia "proposed" to his men that they row out to Prudence and "prevent their landing." Fry's proposal was accepted, and a party of some eighty men from the Kentish Guards rowed the six miles from East Greenwich to Prudence. Fry's men landed early in the morning and immediately began cooking breakfast at their camp on the northern tip of the island. Private Wanton Casey, only fifteen, and a member of the Guards recalled, "While eating breakfast, we received news by a man who ran very fast, that the enemy were landing three or four

[16] Clark, *Naval Documents of the American Revolution: Volume 3*, 767-768: 784. *Providence Gazette,* January 20, 1776. Maytum, "Early Prudence," 79-81. Beaman, *Scituate,* 42. Williams, *Biography of Revolutionary Heroes, 30-32:* 303-305.
[17] Clark, *Naval Documents of the American Revolution: Volume 3,* 784-785. Williams, *Biography of Revolutionary Heroes,* 303-305. Stiles, *Literary Journal,* 654. *Providence Gazette,* January 20, 1776.

miles below us. Our resource was to brave the danger as well as we could." Fry immediately ordered his men into line and with "drums beating and colors flying," marched to engage the British.[18]

Responding to the alarm from General West, fifty men rowed to Prudence from Warren, while a force of eighty men in whaleboats landed at day break on the island. The main force of men from Bristol was led by Captain William Barton of Richmond's Regiment. A pre-war hatter from Warren, he had seen service at Bunker Hill and worked his way to company command. After the burning the night before, the British had returned to their ships. At nine o'clock on the morning of January 13, they returned to continue foraging for supplies and to continue the destruction of the island. From his post on *H.M.S. Rose,* Captain Wallace observed "large bodies of armed Rebels stood behind stone fences to oppose us."[19]

Among those who returned to the fighting on January 13 were Ensign Miller and his men from Richmond's Regiment. Due to a lack of boats at Warwick Neck, few men responded from Colonel Waterman's forces. Perhaps because Wallace's ultimate intentions were unknown, the majority of Rhode Island forces remained on the mainland, ready to defend Providence, which was believed to be Wallace's next objective. Captain Barton deployed his men and waited for the British approach. A British patrol that "strayed too far from the Main Body, fell into an Ambush," as the Marines and sailors attacked a picket post manned by Lieutenant John Carr. Soon a "smart engagement ensued" that resulted in the deaths of three British.[20]

---

[18] Greene, *East Greenwich,* 183-184.

[19] Williams, *Biography of Revolutionary Heroes, 1-32.* Field, *Revolutionary Defenses,* 16-18. Clark, *Naval Documents of the American Revolution: Volume 3,* 784-785.

[20] Clark, *Naval Documents of the American Revolution: Volume 3,* 784-785. *Providence Gazette,* January 20, 1776. Field, *Revolutionary Defenses, 60-63.* Williams, *Biography of Revolutionary Heroes, 30-32: 303-305.* Walker, *So Few the Brave,* 11-22: 122-123.

The fighting raged for nearly three hours on Prudence as Captain Barton led the American forces near Farnham's Farm. Captain Tyringham Howe, the master of *H.M.S. Glasgow* "Observ'd an irregular fire between the Rebels & our people." The *Providence Gazette* reported, "The enemy several times sent out flanking parties, which were as often drove back to their main body." In the fighting, Captain Billings Throop, commanding a company in Richmond's Regiment was mortally wounded; he died on January 25, 1776. Another of Billings's men, Private Job Greenman took a bullet to the left leg. In all, Barton lost one officer and one private mortally wounded, three men wounded, and one man captured. Although outnumbered, these Americans were literally fighting on their own soil and put up a vigorous effort to drive the British back to their ships. From Newport, Dr. Stiles heard "fireing all the afternoon." After talking to several Newport men who were in the engagement, he wrote in his diary. "Our men fought bravely, repulsed & routed the whole Body tho' they had nearly surrounded them on each flank."

After three hours of heavy skirmishing, British forces retreated back to their ships. After the fighting, the Rhode Islanders discovered two British Marines dead on the field, and another wounded who was taken prisoner. However, "they likewise carried off a number of killed and wounded, particularly an officer, that appeared to be badly wounded." The *Providence Gazette* reported, "Our officers and men behaved with the greatest gallantry, and had there been boats at Warwick to carry over the reinforcements from thence, it is thought the enemy's whole party would have been killed or taken."[21]

Ensign James Miller, who had been in the action both days recalled nearly sixty years later, "It was never ascertained how many were killed or wounded, but from the traces of blood it was supposed the enemy suffered some loss in their retreat, pursued as they were by an incessant fire to their ships." Besides losing several men, all that Wallace's squadron found on Prudence were 100 sheep and several bushels of potatoes. After the battle,

---

[21] Stiles, *Literary Journal,* 654-657. *Providence Gazette,* January 20, 1776. Williams, *Biography of Revolutionary Heroes,* 30-32: 303-305.

from his headquarters in Newport, General William West received intelligence from a man named Slocum who was released by the British that "Capt Wallace is very sick of his Voyage to Prudence, having lost fourteen Men kill'd & a number Wounded- They Buried Several on Hope Island. I'm informed Nine were found buried there in one Grave. Two of the wounded are since dead & buried on Rose Island." Captain Wallace, the Royal Navy, and British Marines paid a heavy price for their expedition to Prudence Island. As is typical of many Revolutionary War engagements, the total number of casualties sustained by both sides will never fully be known. Wallace wrote, "Our loss would have been less, had our people have had less spirit."[22]

On January 15, the British returned to Prudence. In the two days since the action of January 13, Wallace anchored off Hope Island where he obtained wood and other supplies. On the fifteenth, Wallace completed his destruction of the island, burning a windmill, six houses, and a number of out buildings. Despite having a large presence in the area, no Rhode Island Militia troops rowed out to the island to engage Wallace. For the rest of the Revolution, Prudence would remain a deserted island. After the occupation of Newport in December 1776, occasional British parties would visit the island to forage for supplies. On December 4, 1777 another skirmish on the island resulted in the deaths of three British Marines.[23]

Even after receiving a blooding at Prudence Island, Wallace remained in Narragansett Bay for several days. He continued to press for supplies, which were given by Loyalists in the town. After receiving news of the American defeat at Quebec, a number of "Friends to the Ministerial Forces in Newport, appear more open & Bold than heretofore, by endeavoring to inflame the Minds of the Inhabitants of the Town." General West did his best to stamp out these Loyalist feelings as he tried to persuade the General Assembly to let him remove "Obnoxious Inhabitants"

---

[22] Williams, *Biography of Revolutionary Heroes,* 303-305. *Providence Gazette,* January 20, 1776. Clark, *Naval Documents of the American Revolution: Volume 3,* 767-768: 954-955.
[23] Maytum, "Early Prudence," 79-80.

from the island. West complained, "Those persons give us more Trouble than Wallaces whole Fleet & as much Danger is to be expected of them." Eventually a number of Loyalists were removed from Newport and sent to Glocester in rural western Rhode Island under General West's personal observation.[24]

After having his forces bloodied at Prudence, and with the siege of Boston continuing, Wallace's squadron was recalled to Boston for refitting and eventual service elsewhere in the American theatre. For nearly two years, Captain Wallace had "kept the Inhabitants of that Province in so much Awe." He had performed valuable service gathering supplies largely from the populace of Newport loyal to the British cause, while attempting to keep Narragansett Bay closed to American privateers. When he decided to attempt to gather supplies from Prudence however, Wallace and his men ran headlong into a determined band of Rhode Island Militia who would not give in to his demands. Admiral Molyneux Shuldham praised his subordinate's service in Rhode Island. "Captain Wallace's services deserve every reward can be confer'd on him, I humbly recommend sending him out in a Larger and better ship."[25]

Captain James Wallace utterly destroyed Prudence Island. Once a vibrant farming community, his forces "agriculturally left the island a wreck." Nearly every dwelling on the island was destroyed, with only "a mass of blackened ruins" remaining, while all the livestock had either been carried off or taken by the British. Many families never returned to the island. The Rhode Island General Assembly heard the pleas of the islanders and repaid twenty families for the loss of crops and livestock, as well as home goods such as tools and other items taken by the British. In addition, claims were filed for the homes destroyed on the island by the British. While this money repaid them for some of the items lost during the burning, it was little compensation for the lives

---

[24] Clark, *Naval Documents of the American Revolution: Volume 3,* 954-955. Sidney S. Rider, ed. *The Diary of Thomas Vernon: A Loyalist, Banished from Newport by the Rhode Island General Assembly in 1776.* (Providence: S.S. Rider, 1881), 1-18.
[25] Roelker, "Patrol of Narragansett Bay," (April 1950), 56-58.

shattered by the destruction of the island. It was only by 1870 as Prudence Island developed into a popular summer retreat did the island regain the population lost during the Revolution.[26]

The Battle of Prudence Island had a profound impact on the lives of the participants. Captain William Barton was promoted to major for his actions on January 13. On July 10, 1777 he again distinguished himself leading a raid in Newport that resulted in the capture of British commander General Richard Prescott. Severely wounded in a skirmish in Bristol in 1778, he would end the war as a colonel. The town of Barton, Vermont was named in his honor.[27]

Captain Knight was also promoted to major for his actions at Prudence Island. He remained in the field throughout the Revolution and saw service at the Battle of Rhode Island in 1778. He attained command of the Third Providence County Regiment and later was actively involved in town politics, serving many years on the town council, while also running a tavern. When Lieutenant Colonel Knight died in 1825 at the age of eighty-five, he was still remembered as "Scituate's bravest son."[28]

In conclusion, the two engagements on Prudence Island on January 12 and January 13, 1776 were decisive for the Patriot cause. Although the British would invade Newport in December 1776 and remained for three years, they were never able to use their base in Newport in which to conduct further raids into the interior of New England. The engagement at Prudence gave the British knowledge of the fighting prowess of the Rhode Island Militia that they would violently defend their state against incursions. The few times that British forces did leave Rhode Island, for raids on Bristol, Warren, and elsewhere, militia forces

---

[26] Maytum, "Early Prudence," 83-85. Revolutionary War Claims, Prudence Island, Rhode Island State Archives.
[27] William West to Rhode Island General Assembly, January 28, 1776, Rhode Island State Archives. For the best sketch on the life of Colonel Barton, refer to Christian M. McBurney, *Kidnapping the Enemy: The Special Operations to Capture Generals Charles Lee & Richard Prescott.* (Yardley, PA: Westholme, 2014)
[28] Beaman, *Scituate,* 41-45. *Providence Gazette,* March 9, 1825.

always turned out in force, with little damage done by Crown troops. Furthermore, the British were never fully able to seal off Narragansett Bay to American privateers who used Providence as a base throughout the war.

For the Rhode Island Militia, Prudence Island was the first engagement for many of these men. For the remainder of the Revolution, they would remain constantly on alert, guarding the shores of Narragansett Bay. In the 1778, thousands of militiamen responded and some were engaged in the Battle of Rhode Island on August 29, 1778. Furthermore, the events at Prudence showed the value of the alarm and beacon system that was common throughout much of New England that led to the overwhelming militia response. Although Prudence Island was thoroughly ravaged by the war, displacing many families and leaving the island a shell of its former self, the men of the Rhode Island Militia were able to give the British yet another defeat on the long road to independence.[29]

---

[29] While many books have been written on Rhode Island's role in the American Revolution, the most pertinent for this study in Christian M. McBurney, *The Rhode Island Campaign.* (Yardley, PA: Westholme, 2011). For an excellent British perspective of operations in Rhode Island refer to Frederick Mackenzie, *The Diary of Frederick Mackenzie.* (New York: New York Times, 1968)

Chapter Two:

"Died in the Service of his Country:"

A new look at Rhode Island Civil War deaths

Civil War historians have long quoted that 620,000 American soldiers, North and South died in the Civil War or as a result of their service. In 2012, Dr. David Hacker of Binghamton University, using the latest available data, stunned the Civil War community by announcing that the casualty figure is actually much higher, nearly 750,000 Union and Confederate military dead. Based on census data, a careful look at the casualty rates among black and immigrant soldiers, and a review of filed pension applications; Dr. Hacker's figure is widely gaining ground in the field as the true number of men who died as a result of their service. For the record, this historian agrees with Dr. Hacker's figure, however, the true number will never be known.[1]

In my research on Rhode Island's role in the Civil War, I have long had a nagging suspicion that the state lost far more men than originally claimed. According to Lieutenant Colonel William F. Fox in his massive *Regimental Losses in the American Civil War,* Rhode Island furnished 23,236 men to serve in the war. It is important to note that this figure includes all Rhode Island enlistments and not just those native-born Rhode Islanders who signed up; many men, most notably those who served in the Fourteenth Rhode Island as well as the Second Rhode Island Cavalry came from other states. Of these, according to Fox, 460 men were killed in action or mortally wounded and 861 died "from all other causes," including of disease, as prisoners of war, and in accidents for a total of 1,321 military deaths during the war.

---

[1] *New York Times,* April 2, 2012.

In his book, Fox offered a stern warning to future scholars regarding Civil War casualty figures. "Days, and often weeks, have been spent on the figures. It is hoped that before disputing any essential fact, a like careful examination of the records will be made." Despite Colonel Fox's statements, it is worth revisiting Rhode Island's Civil War casualty figures.[2]

In his 1964 book, *History of the Rhode Island Combat Units in the Civil War,* General Harold Barker, a veteran of the First and Second World Wars, whose grandfather had served in the Civil War recorded a total of 1,685 men from Rhode Island units who died as a result of their Civil War service. Because he did not footnote his book, it is unclear how General Barker reached this conclusion.[3]

Immediately after the Civil War, the Rhode Island General Assembly appointed a committee of prominent Rhode Islanders, including Ambrose Burnside and John Russell Bartlett to find and accept a proposal for a statewide monument that would list the names of every Rhode Islander who died in the "wicked Rebellion." The monument, officially the Rhode Island Soldiers and Sailors Monument, would be inscribed, "Rhode Island pays tribute to the memory of the brave men who died that their country might live." After a year-long search, the committee settled on a design from Randolph Rogers, consisting of a statue of "America Militant," four bronze panels representing War, Victory, Peace, and History, as well as four additional figures representing the infantry, cavalry, artillery, and navy. Most importantly were the twelve panels that would contain the names of every Rhode Islander who died in the war. The entire monument cost 50,000 dollars and was dedicated in Exchange Place (Kennedy Plaza) on September 16, 1871 to much fanfare.[4]

---

[2] William F. Fox, *Regimental Losses in the American Civil War: 1861-1865.* (Albany: Albany Publishing Company, 1889), preface, 526, 533.
[3] Harold R. Barker, *History of the Rhode Island Combat Units in the Civil War: 1861-1865.* (Providence: NP, 1964), 307-308.
[4] For more on the Rhode Island Soldiers and Sailors Monument, refer to *Report on the Committee on a Monument to the Rhode Island Soldiers and Sailors who perished in suppressing the Rebellion Made to the*

The first step in the monument process was carefully going through the records held by the adjutant general of Rhode Island and compiling a listing of the names to be inscribed on the bronze panels. This in and of itself was an arduous task. When he inherited the records in the early 1890's Elisha Dyer Jr., himself a Civil War veteran and the adjutant general complained about the terrible condition of Rhode Island's Civil War records, "The old and valuable records of the Rhode Island Regiments were being irreparably injured by the constant handling of those who were obliged to refer to them for information. From the close of the war until June, 1883, the records were kept in paste-board boxes in an open bookcase in the Adjutant-General's office, where they were easily accessible to the public, and, consequently, also in danger of being carried off and lost, as well as being spoiled or destroyed by careless handling."[5]

The committee only had a year to go through the thousands of muster rolls, as well as compiling a listing of men from Rhode Island who had served in the Regular service or in units from other states. Despite this momentous task, the committee completed its task and recorded the names of 1,771 Rhode Islanders who died of wounds, disease, in prisons, of

General Assembly, January Session, 1867. (Providence: Providence Press, 1867) and *Proceedings at the Dedication of the Soldiers and Sailors Monument in Providence.* (Providence: A. Crawford Greene, 1871)

[5] Elisha Dyer, *Annual Report of the Adjutant General of the State of Rhode Island and Providence Plantations for the Year 1865. Corrected, Revised, and Republished in Accordance with the Provisions of Chapters 705 and 767 of the Public Laws. Volume I* (Providence: E.L. Freeman, 1893), i. This book, the official listing of Rhode Island's Civil War soldiers is more commonly referred to as *The Revised Register of Rhode Island Volunteers.* Volume One covers those who served in the infantry, while Volume Two covers the cavalry, artillery, Regulars, and U.S. Navy. In the mid-1990s Kenneth Carlson of the Rhode Island State Archives began a meticulous project to finally catalog all of the Civil War papers from Rhode Island. Today, the papers, at the Rhode Island State Archives contain the best records of Rhode Island's Civil War soldiers.

accidents in the service, or of disease immediately upon returning home from the army. These 1,771 names were inscribed upon the monument in Providence. Many names were missed however.[6]

So, who is to be believed? Fox widely regarded as the leading authority on Civil War statistics, or the adjutant general's office in Rhode Island, who was responsible for recording the deaths of Rhode Island's soldiers and sailors. The discrepancy between Fox's figures and those of the state are 450. When one deducts Rhode Islanders who served in the units of other states, as well as in the U.S. Army, U.S. Navy, and Marine Corps, Rhode Island still records a figure of 358 military deaths in Rhode Island regiments over the usually quoted number given by Fox. The question is who is to be believed. In the opinion of this historian, the higher number, quoted by the State of Rhode Island in the 1869, the very names that were inscribed on the Soldiers and Sailors Monument are the correct figure. But a deeper question remains, is the figure of 1,771 Rhode Islanders dying as a result of their Civil War service an accurate figure. Could the number be higher?

I have long held suspicion that the number of Rhode Islanders who died as a result of their Civil War service was over 2,000 and I regularly quoted the number in my books and lectures on the Civil War. In 2014, I set out to test my hypothesis, to finally determine the number of Rhode Islanders who died in the Civil War.

I began my study by focusing on the Seventh Rhode Island Volunteers, a regiment that based on my great-great-great uncle Alfred Sheldon Knight's service, I was intimately familiar with. According to Fox, the Seventh sustained a loss of ninety officers and men killed in action and died of wounds, as well as 109 who died "died of disease, accidents, in prison &c." In his

---

[6] *Names of the Officers, Soldiers, and Seamen in Rhode Island Regiment, or Belonging to the State of Rhode Island, and Serving in the Regiments of other States and in the Regular Army and Navy of the United States, who lost their live in the Defence of their Country in the Suppression of the Late Rebellion.* (Providence: Providence Press, 1869)

only other reference to the regiment, Fox stated that at the Battle of Fredericksburg the Seventh sustained a loss of eleven dead, 132 wounded and fifteen missing for a total of 158. While acknowledging the limited resources of muster rolls and after-action reports that Fox worked with, I knew these figures were woefully low.[7]

Based on a survey of records which have included entries in soldier's letters and diaries, cemetery records, pension files, town clerk death listings; pretty much every scrap of paper that exists regarding the Seventh Rhode Island Volunteers, I determined that the Seventh, which carried a total of 1,179 men on its roles during the war sustained a loss of 104 officers and men who died in combat or of wounds sustained in battle, as well as 109 who died of other causes such as disease and accidents.

Not included in my figures are the twenty-seven men from the Seventh who died after being mustered out of the army, but whose deaths are directly attributable to their Civil War service. Among them is Lieutenant Colonel Job Arnold of Providence. He was discharged for disability in May 1864 after contracting malaria in Mississippi. Arnold died in Providence in December of 1869, and as reported in local papers, he died as a direct result of his service in the Seventh Rhode Island in the Deep South.[8]

Countering Fox's claim regarding the Seventh's losses at Fredericksburg, my determination is the regiment lost three officers and forty-six men killed in action or mortally wounded, as well as 145 officers and men wounded; in addition, three men

---

[7] Fox, *Regimental Losses,* 434:473.
[8] *Manufacturers and Farmers' Journal,* January 3, 1870 and *Newport Mercury,* January 1, 1870. William P. Hopkins, *The Seventh Regiment Rhode Island Volunteers in the Civil War: 1862-1865.* (Providence: Snow & Farnum, 1903), 322. As stated above, my recording of casualty figures has been exhaustively researched from all available soldier's letters and journal entries, pension and service files at the National Archives, death listings in town hall records, as well as cemetery visits.

were captured. This is a total of 197 officers and men of the roughly 570 who went into the fight.[9]

Because of the gruesome nature of Civil War combat, where minie balls and exploding artillery rounds left mangled corpses scattered around the ground, many men were simply listed as missing in action or deserted, leaving families searching, in some cases for years, as to what happened to their family member. On September 17, 1862, the Fourth Rhode Island advanced into Otto's Cornfield at the Battle of Antietam. Forming the extreme left flank of the Army of the Potomac, the Rhode Islanders were flanked in the dense corn and disintegrated under fire. According to one veteran from the regiment, "our men fell like sheep at the slaughter." After a few disjointed volleys, the men of the Fourth fled for their lives. According to the official regimental report field five days after the battle by Lieutenant Colonel Joseph B. Curtis, the regiment lost twenty-one killed, seventy-seven wounded, and two men missing in action. These figures have long been substantiated as the toll of battle for the Fourth on that terrible day.[10]

One of the Fourth's veterans who fell that day was Corporal Austin A. Perkins of Richmond, RI. According to veteran George H. Allen in his 1887 book *Forty-Six Months in the Fourth Rhode Island Volunteers,* Perkins "deserted at Antietam." In a copy of Allen's book held in the archives of Providence College are numerous margin notes obviously written by a veteran

---

[9] Zenas R. Bliss, *The Reminiscences of Major General Zenas R. Bliss: 1854-1876.* Edited by Thomas T. Smith, Jerry D. Thompson, Robert Wooster, and Ben E. Pingenot. (Austin: Texas State Historical Association, 2007), 324-330. Hopkins, *Seventh Rhode Island*, 47-59. Company A, Seventh Rhode Island Monthly Returns, December 1862, Author's Collection. William P. Hopkins gave the Seventh's casualty figures as thirty-nine dead and 120 wounded for a total loss of 159. My figure includes men who later died of wounds and those whose injuries were recorded in myriad of sources including newspapers, letters, journals, and pension records.

[10] Joseph B. Curtis to William Sprague, September 22, 1862, Rhode Island State Archives. *Providence Journal,* September 25, 1862.

of the Fourth who double checked all of Allen's statistics. In the entry for Corporal Perkins he wrote, "Later believed to have been killed at Antietam Sept. 17, 1862." Fortunately, in the early 1890s, as Elisha Dyer prepared to publish his massive *Revised Register,* it was noted under the entry for Austin "Believed to have been killed in the battle of Antietam." Despite the official nod from the state that this soldier lost his life in combat, as in many cases, no additional names were ever added to the Soldiers and Sailors Monument, as such the name of Corporal Austin A. Perkins is not listed on the monument in Providence. With the hindsight of a century and a half to carefully check all the records, it is now believed that the true casualty count of the Fourth in Otto's Cornfield, including those who later died of wounds was thirty dead seventy-one wounded, and four captured. Furthermore, nineteen men are listed as having "deserted in the face of the enemy." Going into the battle with 247 men, the regiment lost well over half of its strength, percentage wise the most ever lost by a Rhode Island unit in any battle of any war.[11]

If the casualty figures can be so different for just the Seventh Rhode Island, I knew that they would increase as well for the other regiments Rhode Island sent to the war. To begin my research, I drew up a plan to visit every town hall in Rhode Island, in addition to combining with a search through historic cemeteries. I gave myself very limited parameters. The notation of death entered into the ledger by the clerk had to clearly indicate that the man died as a direct result of his Civil War service. In the occupation field, the man would be listed as a "soldier," "volunteer" or "in U.S. Service." Under the heading of death, the notation had to clearly indicate that the man died of wounds or disease he encountered in the army. For example, I encountered in the Cranston records a recently discharged soldier who was run over by a railroad car shortly after returning home; this would not qualify as a Civil War death. In the graveyard search, the

---

[11] George H. Allen, *Forty-Six Months in the Fourth Rhode Island Volunteers.* (Providence: J.A. & R.A. Reid, 1887), 371-389. *Revised Register: Volume One,* 301. *Proceedings at the Dedication,* 9-10. John Michael Priest, *Antietam: The Soldiers Battle.* (Oxford: Oxford University Press, 1994), 277-278: 351.

inscription on the headstone had to clearly indicate a Civil War death, such as the often encountered "Died of disease contracted in the service of his country" or "Died of wounds received in the Battle of…"

Although the Rhode Island General Assembly had required city and town clerks to record births, marriages, and deaths at the local level beginning in 1853, and had even sent books to the clerk offices for this purpose, by the 1860s, the system was still woefully inaccurate. Many such vital records continued to only be recorded in family Bibles. Some clerks such as those in Providence, Scituate, Coventry, and Warwick maintained meticulous records from the time, recording the deaths of men who were residents of the town, but died out of state while on military service, as well as those who died of wounds or disease at home. Indeed, the city clerk in Providence even took the time to record the street and address of where the deceased died. In addition, when a soldier died, he listed their unit. Surprisingly towns such as Burrillville, Glocester, Little Compton, and Westerly, who lost soldiers in the Civil War, and whose death records can be found elsewhere recorded few soldiers between 1861-1865 in their town vital records.[12]

The quest to determine the number of Rhode Islanders who died in the Civil War, specifically those who came home and died of wounds or illness took me to every clerk's office in Rhode Island. During the course of my research into these records, to date, I recorded that the clerks had recorded over 400 soldiers in their records who died in the war; the vast majority of whom died at home of wounds or illness contracted in the service, not in camp or on the battlefield. A good example is Samuel Towne of Battery C, First Rhode Island Light Artillery. He died in North Providence on February 13, 1863 of dysentery "contracted in Chickahominy."[13]

---

[12] Death Records for Burrillville, Coventry, Glocester, Little Compton, Providence, Scituate, Warwick, Westerly, contained in the clerk's offices in those communities.
[13] Register of Death entry for Samuel Towne, 1863 North Providence Death Returns, Pawtucket City Hall, Pawtucket, RI.

It will take years to wade through the records recorded in the search, to cross check names against pension files, as well as those recorded in the *Revised Register of Rhode Island Volunteers*. While the research continues, here are several examples of what this research has uncovered thus far.

Alpheus Salisbury was a married, thirty-year-old weaver from Scituate who served in Company K, Seventh Rhode Island Volunteers. Salisbury was shot in the neck in the Seventh's assault up Marye's Heights at the Battle of Fredericksburg. He was discharged from the service for disability on February 2, 1863 and sent home to Scituate. According to a published medical report filed by local doctor William H. Bowen who treated Salisbury:

> The most prominent symptoms were great pain in the head, frequent vomitings, constipation, and a kind of stupor. The wound in the head had not healed, and on probing it pus and blood were discharged. He learned that several pieces of bone had been taken away since the injury was inflicted. On July 1st, he saw the patient, in consultation with another physician. Pain in the head and vomiting still continued, and there was more perfect unconsciousness. The next morning there was paralysis of the side opposite the wound in the head, with one pupil contracted while the other was dilated, and he was perfectly comatose. He thinks that the wound was the primary and the original cause of death.[14]

Private Salisbury died on July 2, 1863 as a direct result of his injuries sustained at Fredericksburg some seven months earlier; he was buried in the Clayville Cemetery. Federal pension clerks agreed with Dr. Bowen's findings and granted his wife a pension based on the fact that he died of his injuries sustained in government service. Despite the government's findings, the name

---

[14] Joseph K. Barnes, *The Medical and Surgical History of the War of the Rebellion.* (Washington, DC: Government Printing Office, 1875), 201

of Alpheus Salisbury is not recorded on the Soldiers and Sailors Monument in Providence.[15]

Some Rhode Island families lost two of their sons in the service of the Union; one Foster family lost three. Among those who lost two was the Pearce family of Richmond. William and Harvey Pearce enlisted in Battery B, First Rhode Island Light Artillery in March 1862. William quickly fell ill on the Virginia Peninsula and was discharged for disability and sent home on June 30, 1862; Harvey struggled on until March 20, 1863, when he too was discharged for disability. Both men returned to Hopkinton where, according to inscriptions on both headstones, they "died of disease contracted in the U.S. Service during the Great Rebellion." The two Pearce brothers are buried side by side at Wood River Cemetery in Hope Valley, the only indication they died in the service is the inscription upon their now fading headstones. Neither name is inscribed on the monument in Providence, or in the local town records.[16]

The Seventh Squadron of Rhode Island Cavalry is one of the state's more interesting Civil War units. Composed of one company raised from students from Dartmouth and Norwich, and one from men from northern Rhode Island, the squadron spent an uneventful three months of service in the Shenandoah Valley in the summer of 1862. Indeed, the regiment's only glory came in the last days of their enlistment when they participated in a wild breakout from the Harpers Ferry garrison. According to the army records, only one squadron member, Arthur Coombs of Thetford, VT, a student from Norwich died of typhoid when the squadron was stationed near Winchester, Virginia. Another Seventh Squadron casualty was Henry C. Colwell of Glocester. He died of typhoid on November 3, 1862 in Chepachet, a month after returning home from the front. While recorded in the town clerk's

---

[15] Alpheus Salisbury, Pension File, National Archives. *Proceedings at the Dedication,* 55.

[16] Harvey and William Pearce Headstones, Wood River Cemetery, Richmond, RI. *Revised Register: Volume II,* 784. *Proceedings at the Dedication,* 61-62.

records, Colwell's name is not on the Soldiers and Sailors Monument, nor is that of Private Coombs.[17]

Ira E. Cole was seventeen and a farmer from Foster when he enlisted in Company E of the Third Rhode Island Heavy Artillery in the summer of 1861. Assigned to artillery duty in Georgia, Florida, and South Carolina, the Third, like the vast majority of Civil War regiments lost far more men to illness than to the enemy's guns. Private Cole survived his three-year enlistment unscathed. He returned to Foster in the summer of 1864 a sick man however. On August 31, 1865, according to the town clerk's notations, Cole died of "chronic dysentery contracted in camp" at his home in Foster. Like the majority of the men chronicled in this study, his name was not listed as a Civil War death of state authorities.[18]

Perhaps the most interesting find so far in the search has been a remarkable discovery regarding Private Ira Cornell of Coventry, who served in Company K of the Seventh Rhode Island Volunteers. Cornell was a farmer from Coventry who enlisted on August 14, 1862. A day later, his son Ira Cornell Jr. also enlisted. The senior Cornell was wounded at Fredericksburg. According to the official army records, he "deserted at Cincinnati, O. April 1, 1863." His son, Ira Cornell junior was discharged for disability on October 14, 1864 and died of tuberculosis contracted in the army on April 29, 1867 in Coventry.[19]

When I conducted my initial survey of compiling a roster of the Seventh Rhode Island, I listed the senior Cornell as did the

---

[17] Register of Death entry for Henry C. Colwell, 1862 Death Returns, Glocester Town Hall, Chepachet, RI. *Revised Register: Volume II,* 305-310. *Proceedings at the Dedication,* 63-65.
[18] Frederic Denison, *Shot and Shell: The Third Rhode Island Heavy Artillery Regiment in the Rebellion, 1861-1865.* (Providence: J.A. & R.A. Reid, 1879) Register of Death entry for Ira E. Cole, 1865 Death Returns, Foster Town Hall, Foster, RI. *Proceedings at the Dedication,* 50.
[19] Hopkins, *Seventh Rhode Island,* 522. Register of Death entry for Ira Cornell Jr., 1867 Death Returns, Coventry Town Hall, Coventry, RI.

official records, as having deserted. In the back of my mind however, was why a father would desert the army, leaving his teenage son alone in the service? One day this past fall while researching in the Coventry Town Hall, I discovered a notation that literally blew me away. The town clerk in Coventry kept meticulous records of all soldiers who died in the army from the town. As I was busy looking through the register of deaths in Coventry, I saw the name of Ira Cornell. In the margin, the clerk had annotated, "Drowned in the Ohio River in the attempt of crossing it in the line of his duty." This record makes sense, for on that date the steamer *Kentucky,* transferred the Seventh Rhode Island across the Ohio River from Cincinnati to Covington, Kentucky. I have found no reference of the death in any letters from Seventh Rhode Island soldiers recording this, nor is it recorded in the official history of the regiment. Despite this, the Coventry records are highly accurate, and the clerk would have received first-hand information from a fellow soldier or a relative about the death. In addition, there is a grave marker in Pine Grove Cemetery in Coventry for Cornell that gives a date of death of April 1, 1863. In my records of the Seventh Rhode Island I have changed my entry to reflect that Ira Cornell died in the service of his country and did not desert the flag.[20]

Will the number of Rhode Island soldiers who died as a result of battle injuries or of disease contracted in the service ever be known? The answer is probably not. Men immediately left the state after mustering out, some never returned, many never had their deaths recorded in the vital records, and today lie buried in an unmarked grave. The best available data supports that approximately 2,000 Rhode Island soldiers, sailors, and Marines died as a result of their Civil War service, which severely contradicts the previous numbers as being too low.

Perhaps Thomas Williams Bicknell summed it up best in his massive *The History of the State of Rhode Island and Providence Plantations* when describing the Civil War registers from the smallest state: "This report gives the name, date of

---

[20] Register of Death entry for Ira Cornell, April 1, 1863, Coventry Town Hall. Hopkins, *Seventh Rhode Island,* 69-70.

enrollment, dates of mustering in and mustering out, promotions, transfers, or all soldiers and sailors from Rhode Island in the Civil War. Totals are not given and no record as to the nationality, birth, or birth-place of any of the whole number. In most cases the Rhode Island residence is noted. From these data, it is almost impossible to determine how many men Rhode Island contributed to the War. It can safely be stated that the State furnished the full quota of men and supplies that she was called to render."[21]

[21] Thomas Williams Bicknell, *The History of the State of Rhode Island and Providence Plantations: Volume II.* (New York: American Historical Society), 820-821.

Chapter Three:

"The muffled drum's sad roll has beat:"

The first deaths in the Seventh Rhode Island

Today when an American service member is killed overseas it initiates a long process that includes the terrible knock on the door, the repatriation and processing of the deceased to the United States, and the full support of the government helping the family during the very difficult time. During the Civil War and up through Vietnam, no such process was in order. In the Civil War it generally fell to a member of the soldier's company to write a letter home to inform the family of their loved one's death, while the family was responsible to pay the cost of having the remains shipped home. Because of the nature of Civil War deaths and combat, many families never learned what became of their soldier, and searched for years for information about what happened to them. Well over half of all Civil War soldiers buried in National Cemeteries are listed as "Unknown."

Between September 10, 1862 and June 9, 1865, 1,179 men served in the Seventh Rhode Island Volunteers. This includes 954 original members of the regiment, and 226 veterans who transferred in the fall of 1864 from the Fourth Rhode Island Volunteers. Of this number an appalling 104 were killed in combat or died of wounds, and a further 109 died of disease and in accidents in the service. Not counted in the figure is twenty-seven men who died immediately after being mustered out of the service and whose deaths are directly attributable to their service in the Seventh Rhode Island. In heavy fighting at Fredericksburg and the Overland Campaign, and through diseases such as typhoid, dysentery, pneumonia, malaria, and yellow fever, in Virginia, Mississippi, and Kentucky the losses the Seventh sustained were felt in every Rhode Island community. Nearly every Rhode Islander knew someone who died in the Civil War.[1]

One of the ten companies that composed the Seventh Rhode Island Volunteers was Company A. The company of 100 men was raised among the mill workers and farmers of Westerly, Hopkinton, Richmond, and Charlestown in July and August 1862. The men of Company A left behind a rich written record.[2]

After leaving Rhode Island on September 10, 1862, the Seventh spent several weeks in Washington before being sent to join the First Brigade, Second Division of the Ninth Army Corps which was then camped in Pleasant Valley, Maryland, not far from the battlefield at Antietam. Almost immediately upon leaving the state, many of the members of the regiment, including my own great-great-great uncle, Alfred Sheldon Knight of Scituate became ill with diseases such as typhoid, pneumonia, and dysentery caused by poor food and water, overcrowding, and unsanitary conditions.

The first two deaths in the regiment occurred on October 5, 1862 when Charles Baker Greene of Company A, a nineteen-year-old farmer from Ashaway and twenty-one-year-old John F. Brown of Exeter both died of typhoid. Brown passed at a hospital in Washington and Baker died in Frederick, Maryland. Because these first two deaths occurred in hospitals away from the regiment, the soldiers were mourned by their comrades, but the men in the ranks did not experience the loss first hand.[3]

---

[1] Seventh Rhode Island Volunteers, Descriptive Books, Rhode Island State Archives. William P. Hopkins, *The Seventh Regiment Rhode Island Volunteers in the Civil War: 1862-1865.* (Providence: Snow & Farnum, 1903), 311-531. The figures of enlistments and deaths in the Seventh Rhode Island is based on a very, very careful study of all available soldier's letters, town hall records, pension papers, and cemetery visits by this author. These casualty figures are the most comprehensive available to date.
[2] *Narragansett Weekly,* August 7, 1862 and August 21, 1862.
[3] Kris VanDenBossche, ed. *Pleas Excuse All Bad Writing: A Documentary History of Rhode Island during the Civil War Era 1861-*

Immediately upon arrival at Pleasant Valley, a typhoid epidemic erupted through the ranks of the Seventh, sending many to the regimental hospital, while the worst cases were discharged and sent back home to Rhode Island. The Seventh was blessed to have three very competent doctors assigned to it, including Major James Harris who had served as a volunteer surgeon in the Crimean War and had been captured at Bull Run rather than abandon the patients he was treating. Despite the best efforts of these three doctors and Stephen Peckham, a gifted Brown University chemist who acted as the regimental hospital steward, there was nothing this medical team could do to stem the typhoid epidemic. Soon the disease claimed the first victims to die in the Seventh's camp; two privates from Company A.[4]

One of these men was Gideon Franklin Collins, a married farmer from Hopkinton who had enlisted in Company A on August 8, 1862. He was typical of many of the men from rural Rhode Island who had never had exposure to the diseases that were hitting the regiment hard as they adjusted to field service. In a letter of condolence to the family of Charles Baker Greene, one of the Seventh's first victims, Private Edwin R. Allen, later the commander of Company A, wrote on October 15, 1862. "Franklin Collins has been quite sick, but is more comfortable today- he is pale and poor- in the Regimental hospital." Only two months after leaving Hopkinton, he was dead at the age of twenty-four, a victim of the typhoid epidemic spreading throughout the Pleasant Valley camps of the Army of the Potomac. [5]

1865. (Peace Dale, RI: Rhode Island Historical Document Transcription Project, 1993), 62-67. Alfred Sheldon Knight Civil War letters, author's collection.

[4] VanDenBossche, *Please Excuse,* 62-67. Stephen Farnum Peckham, "Recollections of a Hospital Steward in the Civil War," Newport Historical Society, Newport, RI. Hopkins, *Seventh Rhode Island,* 332-335.

[5] Company A, Seventh Rhode Island Volunteers, Descriptive Book, Rhode Island State Archives. VanDenBossche, *Pleas Excuse,* 65-66.

In his, *The Seventh Regiment Rhode Island Volunteers in the Civil War: 1862-1865,* William Palmer Hopkins provided this brief sketch of Collins' life:

> Gideon Franklin Collins, son of Welcome and Sallie Collins, was born in Greenfield, Pa., Oct. 19, 1837, but his boyhood was spent in Hopkinton, R.I. In early life he became an active church member, and lived a consistent life, as his many friends have testified. On a certain day at Camp Bliss he had a fainting fit after which he never was entirely well. His appearance was different, and though he performed all his duties and seemed quite well at times, those periods were brief. Finally, he was obliged to go to the hospital, and it soon became evident he had typhoid fever. Up to within a few days of his death the doctor gave hope of recovery, but it was evident his strength was failing fast. None could be more patient than he. The night before he died he told one of the female nurses that he felt a great change coming over him, yet he remained perfectly composed and happy. He died at Pleasant Valley, Md., Oct. 19, 1862, on his twenty-fifth birthday. He left a widow and one child.[6]

Only the day before, George Washington Gardiner, another twenty-four-year-old Hopkinton private in Company A also died of the disease in the Seventh's camp.

While two soldier's deaths over the course of the war had little impact on the regiment, especially as the toll of the Seventh's service increased, the first fatalities in the regiment's camp hit hard. Collins and Gardiner were well known by their fellow soldiers from Hopkinton, and Colonel Zenas Randall Bliss of Johnston, a West Pointer and the Seventh's commander decided that a fitting ceremony should be held to honor their memory. In his post-war memoirs, he wrote, "It was the first death in our regiment, and I desired to show every possible respect to the deceased, I ordered out the whole regiment and marched it to the

---

[6] Hopkins, *Seventh Rhode Island,* 381.

grave in a little grove and formed it in a square, and the chaplain preached for nearly two hours, till everyone was tired out."[7]

The funeral, the only one ever held as a regiment was long remembered by the men of the Seventh. Charles P. Nye of Richmond wrote home to Benjamin Pendleton in Hopkinton about the event, "The 9th New Hampshire Brass Band led the prosesion to the grave followed by our drum band and thin eighteen of Company A with reverse arms then the cops and then the rest of com. A, than came the whole Regiment with commissioned Officers in the rear the text was taken in the 5 chapter of Jacob 60 verse after the cops was then lowered in to their graves three vollys was fired over their grave and then we returned to our quarters. It was the Solomens sene that I ever witness."[8]

Two days before the Seventh's baptism of fire at Fredericksburg, the *Narragansett Weekly* of Westerly published this letter of condolence to the wife of Private Gideon F. Collins in the December 11, 1862 edition. The editor of the *Weekly* wrote, "The following letter will interest many of our readers, who are acquainted with the write and the subject."[9]

> Pleasant Valley, Md.
> Oct. 21st 1862

Mrs. Gideon F. Collins,-

It becomes my painful duty to inform you of the death of your husbands, which took place on the morning of the 19th instant, at 7 o'clock. I am satisfied that he has never been entirely well, since the day that he had a fainting spell at Camp Bliss. His appearance has been different from what it was before. This is the

---

[7] Zenas R. Bliss, *The Reminiscences of Major General Zenas R. Bliss: 1854-1876.* Edited by Thomas T. Smith, Jerry D. Thompson, Robert Wooster, and Ben E. Pingenot. (Austin: Texas State Historical Association, 2007), 312-313.
[8] Bliss, *Reminiscences,* 312-313. Charles P. Nye to Benjamin Pendleton, October 22, 1862, Rhode Island Historical Society.
[9] *Narragansett Weekly,* December 11, 1862.

opinion of all of the boys who were acquainted with. Sometimes it is true, he seemed pretty well and went through with his duties; but it would be only for a short time.

He was finally obliged about two weeks ago, to go to the hospital, and in a short time, it was evident that he had the typhoid fever. From this time, he had no appetite, and rapidly lost flesh. His fever was apparently light, and slow its operation was but too sure. Up to within a few days of his death, the Doctor[10] gave some encouragement of his recovery; but it was evident that his strength was failing very fast.

The night before he died, while poor George Gardiner, who died in the early part of the night was in his last agonies, Miss Gibson,[11] one of the female nurses, knelt down between them, and offered a fervent prayer for them both. Your husband listened attentively, but said nothing at that time. In the course of the night he told another nurse, that he felt there was a great change, and he appeared to know that he was dying. He was perfectly composed and happy as far as could be ascertained from the few remarks he made. I think I have never seen any one more patient in sickness. One of the surgeons[12] was with him when he died. He told me he

---

[10] Major James Harris of Providence was the regimental surgeon of the Seventh. One of the most respected physicians in the army, he had graduated from Brown and the Philadelphia College of Medicine and Surgery. He served as a volunteer surgeon to the Russian Army in the Crimean War. In 1861 he served as assistant surgeon of the First Rhode Island Detached Militia and was captured at Bull Run rather than abandon his patients. Commissioned into the Seventh Rhode Island, he eventually became the medical inspector of the Ninth Corps. After the war Harris moved to Japan and devoted himself to the study of anthropology; he lived in Japan for the rest of his life and died around 1900, having never returned to the United States. Hopkins, *Seventh Rhode Island,* 332-333.

[11] Unknown. While the Seventh had several male soldiers detailed to its hospital detachment in a role that would today be considered that of a nurse's aide, no female nurse is known to have served in the Seventh. See Peckham, "Recollections of a Hospital Steward."

[12] The two assistant surgeons of the Seventh Rhode Island were Dr. William Alvestus Gaylord of Providence who was a graduate of Harvard

never saw a man die easier; and a lady who was present, told me that he died without a struggle or convulsion. I saw him every day during the latter part of his sickness; sometimes, two or three times a day. I think he longed for home, and the loved ones there; though he would never admit that he was home-sick. But who would not feel home-sick when so reduced in physical strength?

I must say, that the boys were very kind to him-especially Aldrich C. Kenyon[13] and George A. Thomas.[14] In fact he was a favorite among his acquaintances. We buried him and George Gardiner with military honors on the 20th at 4 p.m. The place selected for their graves is on the edge of the woods, north-west from our camp. They lie between two oak trees, about one rod apart, and a beautiful dog-wood spreads its branches over their quiet resting place. Every one I have heard speak of it says that it is a beautiful place for a burial.

The Chaplain, Rev. Mr. Howard,[15] preached from 2 Cor v. 20: "Now then we are ambassadors for Christ," & c. The Chaplain wishes me to assure you of his deepest sympathy; also Capt.

Medical School and Dr. Albert Gallatin Sprague Jr. of Warwick who had attended Jefferson Medical College and had served three months previously in the Tenth Rhode Island. Hopkins, *Seventh Rhode Island,* 333-334.

[13] Aldrich C. Kenyon was a married twenty-seven-year-old farmer from Hopkinton who enlisted on August 7, 1864. Wounded at Bethesda Church on June 3, 1864, he was mustered out on June 9, 1865. After the war he resumed farming in Voluntown, Connecticut where he is buried. Company A Descriptive Book.

[14] George Amos Thomas was a married twenty-eight-year-old blacksmith from Hopkinton who enlisted on August 7, 1864, He died of typhoid on April 14, 1863 at Baltimore, Maryland. Company A Descriptive Book.

[15] Harris Howard, also known as Harris Howard Tinker was the chaplain of the Seventh Rhode Island. A native of Illinois, he was a forty-two-year-old Methodist-Episcopal minister in Providence when the war broke out. Unpopular with the troops, he resigned in July 1863 and later moved to Maine and Kansas City, Missouri where he died of paralysis. Hopkins, *Seventh Rhode Island,* 334. Peckham, "Recollections of a Hospital Steward." Bliss, *Reminiscences,* 312-313.

Leavens[16] and Lieut. Kenyon.[17] Capt. Leavens has taken charge of all valuables your husband had in his possession at the time of his death, as well as of some that he had entrusted to others before he died. He has turned over his knapsack and clothing to the Quartermaster of the regiment,[18] to be paid for when his monthly pay shall be drawn. The other valuables he has sent in Lieut. Inman's trunk.[19] They will be forwarded to T.T. & E Barber of Brand's Iron Works,[20] through whom you will receive them in the time.

---

[16] Lewis Leavens of Hopkinton commanded Company A and recruited the Hopkinton men for the unit. Born in New York City in 1823, by the outbreak of the Civil War he was a mill owner in the village of Canonchet. Slightly wounded at Fredericksburg in December 1862, he resigned his commission and returned to New York City, where he resided for the rest of his life. Hopkins, *Seventh Rhode Island,* 349-350.

[17] David R. Kenyon of Richmond was a twenty-nine-year-old married "manufacturer" who recruited most of the Richmond contingent for Company A. Wounded in the leg at Fredericksburg; he was promoted to captain of Company I, but resigned in March 1863. After the war he continued working in the mill industry, and served in a variety of civic officers; he died in 1897. He is buried in Wood River Cemetery, Richmond. Hopkins, *Seventh Rhode Island,* 349.

[18] The original quartermaster of the Seventh Rhode Island was Lieutenant Dean Smith Linnell of Providence. He had traveled to California during the Gold Rush. Linnell had served in the Tenth Rhode Island in the quartermaster department, and was transferred to the Seventh Rhode Island in August 1862. His commission was revoked by Governor William Sprague in November 1862 and he was replaced by John R. Stanhope of Newport. Linnell returned to Rhode Island and went to New York City and died in a machinery accident there in 1867. Hopkins, *Seventh Rhode Island,* 329-330. Dean S. Linnell Papers, author's collection.

[19] First Lieutenant George B. Inman was a native of Burrillville. A graduate of the State Normal School, he was a teacher when he was commissioned in September 1862 in Company H of the Seventh. Inman was assigned as the commander of the Seventh's wagon train. He resigned shortly after the Battle of Fredericksburg. After the war he moved west and is buried at Fort Leavenworth National Cemetery. Hopkins, *Seventh Rhode Island,* 361.

[20] The village of Brand's Iron Works in Richmond, RI is now known as Wyoming.

Your husband, I believe gave his wallet and money (amounting to five or six dollars) in charge of Aldrich C. Kenyon, who no doubt will account to you for them. I do not know what I can add that would comfort you in your bereavement. It is my fervent prayer, that the Good Shepherd of Israel will be to you a tender husband, and a father to your orphan child; and that you and all of the other relatives and friends, may find that consolation in the gospel which it were vain to look for elsewhere.

Your sincere friend

Joseph W. Morton[21]

Unfortunately, this would be just one of many such letters sent to Hopkinton during the Civil War years, as one out of every six men from the town perished in the war. The remains of Private Gardiner were returned to Hopkinton and buried in the Pine Grove Cemetery in Hope Valley. It is unknown where Private Collins is buried, as he does not have a memorial stone in Hopkinton or a burial in the Antietam National Cemetery.[22]

With the death of her husband, and a young son, Franklin M. Collins, to support, Susan E. Collins knew that she could turn to the government for help under the provisions of the Pension Act of July 14, 1862 granting pensions to the widows and orphans of

---

[21] Second Lieutenant Joseph W. Morton was born on January 3, 1821 in Lawrence County, PA. He became an educator and Seventh Day Baptist minister before the war and in 1859 moved to Hopkinton to become principal of the Hopkinton Academy. Enlisting in August 1862, he became ill with malaria and resigned in December 1862. After returning home he resumed his ministerial duties and moved to the Midwest. He died in Minnesota in 1893. Hopkins, *Seventh Rhode Island,* 368-370.
[22] S.S. Griswold, *Historical Sketch of the Town of Hopkinton: From 1757 to 1876 comprising a period of 119 years.* (Hope Valley: L.W.A. Cole, 1877), 46-51. Gayle E. Waite and Lorraine Tarket-Arruda, *Hopkinton, Rhode Island Historical Cemeteries.* (Baltimore: Gateway Press, 1998), NP, entry HP #4.

volunteers who died in Federal service. She filed on January 9, 1864 and on October 11, 1864 was receiving a small pension of eight dollars per month. Both Captain Leavens and Lieutenant Kenyon wrote affidavits in support of Mrs. Collins' relief. Leavens wrote, "I have no doubt that the fever was contracted from exposure while in the line of his duty in the Service of the United States."

Susan Collins remarried Damon Young of Bristol on September 7, 1870, thus vacating her claim to a pension, while her son continued to receive eight dollars per month until he turned sixteen in 1876. With the death of her second husband, Susan remarried a third time to George T. Collins of Moosup, Connecticut in October 1896; George Collins died in 1903. Neither one of her other husbands served during the Civil War. Under the provisions of a generous Federal pension act in 1903, Civil War widows who had remarried, but whose subsequent spouses had died, could refile a pension claim based on the marriage to the spouse who had died as a result of his Civil War service. As such, Susan, now sixty-seven and living in Ashaway refiled for a pension based on her marriage to Gideon F. Collins in February 1904. Mrs. Collins was again approved and received a Federal pension of twelve dollars per month until her death on May 13, 1915 when she was again "dropped from the rolls."[23]

---

[23] Gideon F. Collins, Pension File, National Archives.

Chapter Four:

Solving a Rhode Island Civil War mystery:

Private Hiram Salisbury Battey

Being a historian is oftentimes compatible to being a detective. You are given a problem and often come up with creative ways to find a solution to that problem. In my career in Federal law enforcement, I have found that my Master of Arts in American History that I obtained from Rhode Island College in 2010 has often given me an edge into solving very complex problems relating to my job. Historians are trained to think critically, analyze facts from different angles, conduct in-depth research, use technology, interview people, give presentations, and write reports; all skills that are compatible to my "day job." In 2012, I was given a problem to solve, and after four years of analyzing the available data, have finally made my conclusions.

Back in the fall of 2012, I was visiting a friend in Rhode Island who is also an antiques dealer in South County. Over the years we have developed a good friendship based on our mutual deep interest in Rhode Island and the Civil War. Being on the front lines of the antique world, he has been able to "pick" a number of high quality items relating to the Seventh Rhode Island Volunteers for me; indeed, one of the items happened to be a photograph of my great-great-great uncle Alfred Sheldon Knight who served in the Seventh.

During this one visit, I purchased some Civil War letters and other odds and ends. He showed me some other items for sale, and one particularly caught my eye. It was a tintype of a young soldier that was photographed from an ambrotype. Having done extensive research on the Civil War, I knew that this was a very common practice for families to create copies of images for a soldier who died in the service. The soldier was unidentified, but my friend said that the image came from an auction in Foster that had a number of items from the Salisbury family in it. He thought the soldier might be from the Third Rhode Island Heavy Artillery, but was unsure. My great-great-great grandmother, Emma Salisbury was from Scituate and had married into my Knight line. Either way, the price was right and I took the image back to Vermont with me, carefully putting it away in the "archives room" for future research. I typically do not buy items that are not identified, but there was something about this picture, a young man who more than likely died in the Civil War.

For nearly a decade I worked on and off on a completing a regimental roster for the Seventh Rhode Island Volunteers. Transcribing the regimental descriptive books from the Rhode Island State Archives in Providence, I added details over the years to the barebones information often found in the "official record" such as battlefield casualties, discharge information, where and how the men died, marital status, occupation, and the town they enlisted from. This data has been gleamed from a wide range of sources such as enlistment papers, pension records, census data, period newspapers, soldier's letters and diaries, as well as cemetery visits. In 2015, I began an ambitious project to document the burial location of every man in the Seventh Rhode Island. I began by "scrubbing" each name through three online databases, namely the Rhode Island Historical Cemetery database, www.findagrave.com, as well as the Sons of Union Veterans of the Civil War burial database at www.suvcwdb.org. Furthermore, I also conducted research using the excellent set of John Sterling cemetery books, town hall visits, as well as my own visits to nearly every Civil War era cemetery in Rhode Island and elsewhere. This ambitious project resulted in finding the burial locations of nearly two thirds of the men in the Seventh Rhode Island Volunteers. While the vast majority was buried in Rhode Island, as well as nearby Connecticut, and Rhode Island, men from the regiment are buried throughout the country, including

50

Washington, Oregon, California, Mississippi, Arkansas, Ohio, Kentucky, and Kansas.

During the search for the burial locations of the men in Company K, I was very interested, as the majority of the men were from Coventry, Foster, and Scituate and these were the graves I flagged every year in my youth as a member of Colonel Zenas R. Bliss, Camp 12, Sons of Union Veterans of the Civil War. Scrubbing the names through the various databases, I recorded that there is a cenotaph for Private Hiram S. Battey at the Atwood-Salisbury Lot, Scituate Historical Cemetery #44, located on Trimtown Road in Scituate. My mind began to think for a minute, Hiram S. Battey, the S. stood for Salisbury, and he was buried in the Salisbury Lot. Battey was seventeen when he died in 1863, a very young soldier.

I started thinking back at that instant to the picture I had bought from my friend. Although he had suggested the man was from the Third Rhode Island Heavy Artillery, I knew better. Based on the type of uniform he was wearing, I knew the man was from the Seventh Rhode Island, as they wore a type of coat with a very tall collar that was peculiar to the regiment. Obviously, the image was one taken from an ambrotype of a soldier who had died in the service. As a detective, I was putting the clues together, dead soldier + Seventh Rhode Island uniform, who could this man be. The final clue was the auction. The tintype had come to auction with a bunch of papers from the Salisbury family. This last clue proved the tipping point. The man in the unknown photograph was Private Hiram Salisbury Battey of Company K, Seventh Rhode Island Volunteers.

Hiram Salisbury Battey was the son of Henry A. and Mary J. (Kingsley) Battey. He was born in Scituate in 1846; his parents had been married in Fall River on December 28, 1828. Because Rhode Island did not require registration of vital records until 1853, many such birth records of the Civil War generation are lost. Some "official" records also claim Hiram was born in Providence. Together the Battey family consisted of five children. In the 1850 Census, Henry and the family were listed as residing in Scituate, with Henry A. listed as a farmer. Ten years later the family was residing in Johnston, not far from Scituate. Fifteen-year-old Hiram was listed as a farm laborer, as were his brothers John and Henry L.[1]

When the Civil War broke out in 1861, the Battey boys volunteered for service. John M. Battey enlisted in Battery E, First Rhode Island Light Artillery on September 30, 1861 and was eventually promoted to corporal. Battery E was recruited primarily in western Rhode Island and contained a very large group of men from Scituate and neighboring Coventry. He served in every major battle with the Army of the Potomac, including Gettysburg; at Chancellorsville he had a harrowing experience behind enemy lines. John survived unscathed and was mustered out October 3, 1864. Henry L. Battey served as a member of Company G, Second Rhode Island Volunteers. He enlisted on January 5, 1865 and saw service in the closing days of the war at Petersburg and Sailor's Creek, John was mustered out July 13, 1865.[2]

In the summer of 1862, Rhode Island was tasked with raising 2, 712 men under Lincoln's call of 300,000 men of July 1, 1862. Although recruiting for the Seventh Rhode Island had begun in May, enlistments lagged. Now under the seriousness of the latest call, the towns of Rhode Island began to offer bounties for men to enlist for three years to serve in the Seventh. While patriotism and the noble idea of freeing the slave were certainly motivating factors, the single greatest pull for men to join the regiment was for the money. Most towns offered bounties of $400, while South Kingstown offered five hundred. As a farm laborer,

---

[1] Henry A. Battey, Declaration for Father's Pension, August 25, 1891, Hiram S. Battey Pension File, National Archives, Washington, DC. 1850 U.S. Census, State of Rhode Island, County of Providence, Town of Scituate, National Archives. 1860 U.S. Census, State of Rhode Island, County of Providence, Town of Johnston, National Archives.
[2] George Lewis, *The History of Battery E, First Regiment Rhode Island Light Artillery, In the War of 1861 and 1865, To Preserve the Union.* (Providence: Snow & Farnum, 1892), 11: 163: 170-172: 215. *Revised Register of Rhode Island Volunteers.* (Providence: E.L. Freeman, 1893). *Volume I,* 85. *Volume II,* 849.

this represented several years' wages for Hiram Battey. Although his exact motivations will never be known, like many comrades, he more than likely saw the dollar figure and decided to enlist. Under this call for men, Scituate was ordered to recruit sixty soldiers. At a special town meeting on July 27, 1862, a bounty of four hundred dollars was to be paid to each man enlisting before August 18 who volunteered for three years; three hundred of that amount would eventually be reimbursed by the state, leaving the taxpayers of Scituate to make up the extra hundred dollars per man. Two hundred was to be paid up front, with the remaining two hundred paid over the term of the enlistment. In all, thirty-two Scituate residents enlisted in the Seventh Rhode Island under this call, while others, like Hiram Battey enlisted in the town and were credited towards Scituate's quota.[3]

Although he was a resident of Johnston at the time, Battey was a native son of Scituate, and joined the local company, enlisting on August 8, 1862 in Scituate. Battey signed his own name to the enlistment papers. Surprisingly, he stated he was eighteen and had been born in Providence; his father later claimed he was born in 1846 in Scituate. The examining surgeon noted that Battey had blue eyes, brown hair, a light complexion, and was five feet four inches tall. These are all physical features seen in the known image of Battey. Because he was underage, Hiram's father Henry A. Battey went to the recruiting office with his son and signed the enlistment form as well to the fact, "I do freely give my consent to his volunteering as a soldier in the Army of the United States for a period of three years."[4]

Company K of the Seventh Rhode Island was recruited primarily from the towns of Coventry, Foster, and Scituate. The overwhelming majority of the men were farmers and mill workers.

---

[3] William P. Hopkins, *The Seventh Regiment Rhode Island Volunteers in the Civil War 1862-1865.* (Providence: Snow & Farnum, 1903), 1-5. *Revised Register: Volume I,* 748-749. *Narragansett Times,* July-August 1862. Minutes of July 27, 1862 and August 22, 1862 Town Meetings, Scituate Town Hall, North Scituate, RI.

[4] Hiram S. Battey, Enlistment Papers, Rhode Island State Archives, Providence, RI.

As the men enlisted, they were forwarded to the village of South Scituate (now under the Scituate Reservoir), where they received a medical exam, uniforms, and were boarded, as well as learning the rudiments of drill and military life. In the third week of August, the company was transferred to Camp Bliss in Cranston, where they joined the rest of the Seventh. Company K had not recruited the fully authorized strength of 100 men. As such, ten men from Richmond and Hopkinton who had enlisted in excess of the quota for Company A were transferred to Company K to bring that company up to full strength.[5]

The Seventh Rhode Island left the state on September 10, 1862 and was assigned to the First Brigade, Second Division, Ninth Corps of the Army of the Potomac, then encamped in Pleasant Valley, Maryland after the bloodbath of Antietam. The men acclimated to army life as disease and desertions began to take a toll on the regiment. The Seventh Rhode Island received their baptism at Fredericksburg on December 13 in the assault on Marye's Heights. In the desperate assault, forty percent of the regiment went down. Company K sustained a loss of four dead and eleven wounded. After the battle, the regiment survived a miserable winter at Falmouth, Virginia where several Scituate soldiers lost their lives to typhoid, dysentery, and pneumonia. Fortunately, Private Battery survived both of these ordeals.[6]

On February 9, 1863 the Seventh left Falmouth and transferred to a new camp with the entire Ninth Corps near Newport News, Virginia. From here the Ninth Corps was sent to Kentucky, performing duty around Lexington and Richmond in April and May 1863. At the same time, General Ulysses S. Grant

---

[5] Patrick Hackett to Parents, August 12, 1862, typescript in author's collection. Seventh Rhode Island Volunteers, Enlistment Papers and Descriptive Books, Rhode Island State Archives.
[6] Hopkins, *Seventh Rhode Island,* 22-49. Zenas R. Bliss, *The Reminiscences of Major General Zenas R. Bliss, 1854-1876.* Edited by Thomas T. Smith, Jerry Thompson, Robert Wooster, and Ben E. Pingenot. (Austin: Texas State Historical Association, 2007), 322-329. Alfred Sheldon Knight to Horace Ralph, December 21, 1862, author's collection.

was laying siege to Vicksburg, Mississippi. In need of reinforcements, the Ninth Corps sailed from Cairo, Illinois to Vicksburg on June 9. While Grant besieged the city, the Ninth Corps reinforcements were posted in a reserve position, and "the time was occupied in throwing up defensive works, to render General Grant's rear perfectly secure."

The Confederates at Vicksburg surrendered on July 4. Immediately after the surrender, a large force, including the Ninth Corps, under the command of William Tecumseh Sherman was dispatched towards Jackson in an attempt to intercept a large Confederate force that had been marching to the relief of Vicksburg. Siege was laid to the city, and on the morning of July 13, the Seventh fought the Battle of Jackson, losing three dead, ten wounded, and two officers captured.[7]

Immediately after the Jackson Campaign, it became clear to Grant that the Ninth Corps had to leave Mississippi. Composed largely of New Englanders, the Ninth Corps began to suffer terribly from the "enfeebling climate." The Seventh left Jackson on July 20 and began marching back to Vicksburg, along the way they took part in looting the plantation of Confederate President Jefferson Davis. Men from the Seventh had begun to die from illness in Mississippi from the start of the campaign; during the march back from Jackson on July 21 Private Joseph H. Holbrook of Glocester simply died by the side of the road and was left by his comrades. Drummer William Palmer Hopkins of Company D wrote of the condition of the Seventh, "Our complexions resemble that of a well-cured ham. Our wardrobes have been sadly reduced. Most are destitute of shoes, many have substituted drawers for trousers, many have shed their shirts. Not a few have arrayed

---

[7] Hopkins, *Seventh Rhode Island*, 76-89. Augustus Woodbury, *Major General Ambrose E. Burnside and the Ninth Army Corps: A Narrative of Campaigns in North Carolina, Maryland, Virginia, Ohio, Kentucky, Mississippi and Tennessee, During the War for the Preservation of the Republic*. (Providence: S.S. Rider & Brother, 1867), 280-286. John K. Hull to Harriet Hull, June 17, 1864, and Edward T. Allen to Benjamin Hull, July 16, 1863, Pettaquamscutt Historical Society, South Kingstown, RI.

themselves in garments foraged along the route. My hat looked as if it had been abandoned as a plaything by a dog." Rations became "musty and wormy" as the men waited nearly two weeks at Milldale, Mississippi for transport ships to take them back up the Mississippi; at the same time, men continued to die or be discharged from the service. Colonel Bliss attributed many of the problems facing the Seventh to the local water of the Yazoo River, which he described as "muddy and hot and full of malaria and fever."[8]

"The men fear if they tarry much longer all will perish from the climate and the poor quality of provisions," wrote one Seventh soldier. Finally, on August 8, the steamer *David Tatum,* "a large but old and shabby craft," arrived to the Seventh's brigade back north. The ship was grossly overloaded, while the doctors and medical staff did as much as possible to treat the sick. Four men from the Seventh Rhode Island died on the ten-day voyage back to Cairo; they were buried along the banks of the Mississippi. Writing in the third person, Drummer Hopkins wrote of his experience with Yazoo Fever, which inflicted many men in the regiment, "He suddenly felt cold and chilly, his head ached, his face became pale, he tried to vomit but could not. Flashes of fever followed. Muscles and joints seemed bruised and lame. He staggered as if intoxicated. In one brief hour it was evident to all the grim disorder had him in firm grasp." Fortunately, Hopkins recovered, and spent much of his life writing a history of the regiment. Finally, on August 20, 1863 the Seventh Rhode Island arrived back in Cincinnati.[9]

Arriving back at Cincinnati after the Mississippi Campaign, the Seventh was in no condition to perform any duty. The men "staggered out of the cars in all stages of emaciation, many barefooted and all scantily attired." At the start of the campaign, Colonel Bliss weighed 267 pounds, three months later

---

[8] Stephen Farnum Peckham, "Reminiscences of a Hospital Steward in the Civil War," Newport Historical Society, Newport, RI. Woodbury, *Ninth Corps,* 286-288. Hopkins, *Seventh Rhode Island,* 116-120. Bliss, *Reminiscences,* 347-350.
[9] Hopkins, *Seventh Rhode Island,* 120-122.

he weighed 189, having lost seventy-eight pounds in the sub-tropical Vicksburg Campaign. As the Seventh and the rest of the Ninth Corps arrived back in Ohio, General Ambrose Burnside was preparing for a campaign in East Tennessee, and intended to take the bulk of the Ninth Corps with him. When a staff officer asked for a report on the condition of the Seventh Rhode Island, Assistant Surgeon Albert G. Sprague wrote, "On our arrival at Cincinnati from our campaign in Mississippi we had but seventy-eight men fit for duty + since that time the health of the regiment has been very poor." Based on the reports from the regimental surgeons, the Seventh did not make the march to Tennessee; rather they were assigned to garrison duty in Lexington, Kentucky where they rebuilt their strength during the fall of 1863.[10]

The Mississippi Campaign was perhaps the greatest ordeal that the Seventh Rhode Island incurred during their service. The tropical diseases such as malaria, yellow fever, Yazoo fever, typhoid, dysentery, and others reduced the regiment to a shell of what it once was. Scores of men received discharges for the illness they suffered, others were transferred to the Veterans Reserve Corps, while nearly sixty members of the regiment died of the illness they contracted in the deep south; only three men from the regiment lost their lives to combat in Mississippi, all suffered during the Battle of Jackson on July 13. The illness' afflicted the men for years afterwards, and was the basis for many pension claims. Lieutenant Colonel Job Arnold was one such man. Discharged for disability in May 1864, he returned home to Providence, suffering in agony for nearly five years, before dying in Providence on December 28, 1869 as a direct result of the diseases he brought back from Mississippi.[11]

---

[10] Hopkins, *Seventh Rhode Island,* 126. Bliss, *Reminiscences* 347-350. Albert G. Sprague to "Captain Woodward," October 30, 1863, James Harris Papers, Rhode Island Historical Society, Providence, RI. James Harris to James Rivers, November 11, 1863, James Harris Papers, Rhode Island Historical Society.
[11] Job Arnold Pension File, National Archives, Washington, DC. *Providence Journal,* December 29, 1869. Seventh Rhode Island Descriptive Book.

Perhaps Private William Henry Jordan who hailed from the hamlet of Hopkins Hollow in western Coventry and served with Battey in Company K of the Seventh best summed up the Mississippi Campaign for the Seventh Rhode Island:

> The whole brigade does not begin to be as large as our regiment was when we came out. It is enough to make the icy chillness creep over one to think of the fearful rate that the men are dying off but it is thought that they are rather in a gain, if anything. Our men are strewn all over the United States most and we have laid many to rest in many different places and in different parts of different states. Some have been lain away in the forest where their graves will never more be seen. Some have been buried in the dead hours of night by the light of a lantern while loved ones at home were perhaps having fond dreams of their loved ones.[12]

In 1908, the veterans of the Seventh Rhode Island Volunteers returned to Vicksburg and dedicated an impressive monument to commemorate the deeds of the regiment in the Mississippi Campaign.[13]

During the Mississippi Campaign, the Ninth Corps Artillery Brigade had been particularly hit hard. The corps historian wrote, "There were not able men enough belonging to the batteries to water and groom the horses." When light artillery batteries were in need of men, they were often allowed to draft recruits from neighboring infantry regiments to temporarily fill up their ranks. Many infantrymen, weary from walking, often jumped at this chance, as it would allow them opportunities to ride horses or sit on the gun carriages. Hiram Battery was one of a few

---

[12] William H. Jordan to Parents, September 4, 1863, author's collection.
[13] Nathan B. Lewis and William P. Hopkins, letter to Commissioner Rigby, 1903-1908, Vicksburg National Military Park, Vicksburg, MS. Seventh Rhode Island Volunteers Veteran's Association Scrapbooks, author's collection.

Seventh Rhode Island men who volunteered for this duty. He was assigned to Battery E, Second United States Artillery.[14]

In the end, Hiram Salisbury Battey could not escape the fate suffered by eleven other men from Company K, Seventh Rhode Island during the Mississippi Campaign. On August 16, 1863 Private Battey died of dysentery at the Marine Hospital in Cincinnati, Ohio. Because he was on detached duty, Captain George A. Wilbur of Company K, who nearly died himself from an illness as contracted in Mississippi, handled the final paperwork. Battey's pay was sent home to his parents, along with notification of his death. Private Hiram S. Battey was laid to rest in grave 521 at Spring Grove National Cemetery in Cincinnati, Ohio. Unfortunately for Battey, his grave was marked as a member of the Regular Army, and not as a soldier of the Seventh Rhode Island Volunteers.[15]

His death was recorded in the Scituate town clerk's records, the clerk noting he was single white male whose occupation was that of a soldier and he died in Kentucky; no cause of death was listed. Oddly enough, the town clerk recorded Hiram as being born in Providence, rather than in Scituate. In time, a cenotaph was erected to his memory in the Joshua Battey Lot in Scituate, Scituate Historical Cemetery #208. At an unknown date the memorial was transferred, along with the remains of other Battey family members to Scituate Historical Cemetery #44, the Atwood Salisbury Lot. Today, the lot is in very poor condition, and despite a thorough search, the cenotaph could not be located.[16]

---

[14] Woodbury, *Ninth Corps,* 288-289. John H. Rhodes, *The History of Battery B, First Regiment Rhode Island Light Artillery in the War to Preserve the Union, 1861-1865.* (Providence: Snow & Farnum, 1894), 1-2: 336. Hiram S. Battery, Company K, Seventh Rhode Island Descriptive Book.

[15] Peckham, "Reminiscences." Company K, Seventh Rhode Island Descriptive Book. Hiram S. Battey, Service File, National Archives. Most of the dead from Company K were from Foster and Scituate.

[16] Record of Deaths in the Town of Scituate, 1863, Scituate Town Clerk's Office.

It is surprising to note, that although he was a native of Scituate and enlisted from Scituate, the name of Hiram S. Battey was not inscribed on the town's Civil War monument dedicated in 1913 "To the Loyal Men of Scituate, 1861-1865." Battey is not remembered in the town he was residing in prior to the Civil War either, as Johnston never erected a Civil War monument. His name was recorded however on the Soldiers and Sailors Monument in Providence in 1871.[17]

Mary J. Battey, Hiram's mother died on April 9, 1872 in Scituate, leaving Henry A. Battey a widower; he did not remarry. As Henry aged, he was not supported by his four surviving children. After Hiram's death, he had moved around the state, residing at different times in Pascoag, Centreville, Coventry, and South Kingstown. By 1891 however, Henry was living back in Scituate. In a rare move, he filed a claim for a dependent father's pension on August 25, 1891 claiming that his son Hiram had supported him with some of his pay while he was in the army. Pension officials were quick to request additional evidence regarding his relationship to Hiram. Henry wrote:

> I was married to Mary Jane Kingsley the mother of the soldier Hiram S. Battey at Fall River Mass. On the 28th day of December 1828, that there is no church or public record of said marriage to my knowledge. The city clerk of Fall River mass informed me that the marriage was not recorded there. That the officiating clergyman is dead and I do not remember who were witnesses to the marriage. My son (the soldier) was born in Scituate, R.I. and there is no church record thereof and no record in Scituate town records. That the physician attending his birth is dead. I do not know where to find two persons who remember the fact of his birth. I have no family record of his birth or death. I have three sons to wit: John M. Battey, Hiram S.

---

[17] Gideon A. Burgess, *The Owen Soldiers Monument.* (North Scituate: E.F. Sibley, 1913). *Proceedings at the Dedication of the Soldiers and Sailors Monument in Providence, to which is Appended a list of the Deceased Soldiers and Sailors whose Names are Sculptured upon the Monument.* (Providence: A. Crawford Greene, 1871), 54.

Battey, and Henry L. Battey who served in the late rebellion. I am an old man and a pension will be a great help to me.[18]

Fortunately for Battey, Congress passed a very liberal pension act in 1890. The Grand Army of the Republic issued a circular stating, "While not just what we asked for, it is the most liberal pension measure ever passed by any legislative body in the world, and will place upon the rolls all the survivors of the war whose conditions of health are not practically perfect."[19]

Although he did not serve, the pension bureau obviously considered Henry A. Battey a survivor of the war. Henry found a neighbor, Anson M. Barr to attest to his statements. As such, he was placed on the pension rolls in 1892. Henry did not have long to enjoy his twelve dollars per month pension; he was dropped from the rolls June 4, 1895 due to his death.[20]

In conclusion, establishing that my mystery photo is that of Private Hiram Salisbury Battey of Company K, Seventh Rhode Island Volunteers has been one of the highlights in my decade and a half of study on this regiment. Using the available clues, conducting in-depth research, and old-fashioned detective skills have proved to be of great use in this case. Once unidentified simply as a member of the Salisbury family, this small photograph now properly identified takes a prominent position in my collection as that of a member of the Seventh Rhode Island who gave his life to his country due to the horrors of the Vicksburg Campaign.

---

[18] Henry A. Battey, Declaration, March 5, 1892.

[19] Stuart C. McConnell, *Glorious Contentment: The Grand Army of the Republic, 1865-1900.* (Chapel Hill: University of North Carolina Press, 1992), 122-152.

[20] Henry A. Battey, Declaration, March 5, 1892. Anson M. Barr, Affidavit, January 29, 1892, Battey Pension File. Pensioner Drop Document, June 4, 1895, Battey Pension File.

Chapter Five:

"An officer of rare judgement:"

Job Arnold

Occasionally I receive an e-mail from a descendant of a Seventh Rhode Island soldier and it is always a delight to see what research their family has done on the soldier. In addition, I am also happy to share my research on the regiment with the family member. One day out of the blue I received an e-mail from Meredith Dyer Sweet of Long Island, Maine. I was quite familiar with Meredith's home as nearly every summer I visit the wonderful Fifth Maine museum on nearby Peak's Island. It turned out that Meredith is a direct descendent of Lieutenant Colonel Job Arnold of the Seventh Rhode Island. We have exchanged many e-mails and Meredith has added greatly to my knowledge of Arnold and the Seventh.

In my study of the regiment, I have been fortunate to obtain a remarkable collection of artifacts, letters, and photographs used and written by members of the Seventh Rhode Island. These items have increased my knowledge of the Seventh, and have greatly assisted in my own research and writing about the regiment. Among these prized relics is a photograph of Lieutenant Colonel Job Arnold of the Seventh Rhode Island Volunteers. What I enjoy the most about studying the Seventh is getting to know the individual soldiers of the regiment. Each man who served left behind a story. By studying one regiment, I have been able to gain a better understanding of the Civil War as it was experienced by this one group of Rhode Islanders. Thanks to the family papers that Meredith has shared with me, I have been able to gain a better understanding of one of the Seventh's most respected officers.

Job Arnold was born on January 18, 1827 in Smithfield, Rhode Island. He received an "ordinary education" in the schools of Providence and spent several years of his youth in New York City. Before the war, Arnold was a jeweler in Providence, and also owned a small farm in Smithfield, where he passed his summers. He was among the first Rhode Islanders to enlist, volunteering for service on April 17, 1861 as part of Company C, First Rhode Island Detached Militia. Arnold was very good friends with James Shaw, who served in the Civil War as lieutenant colonel of the Tenth and Twelfth Rhode Island; he later served as a brigade commander in the United States Colored Troops. Arnold wrote home frequently to Shaw about his service.[1] Arnold wrote why he enlisted:

> I never was ambitious of military glory- simple duty- the consciousness that the time had arrived when our Country needed the best exertions- ie the lives if need be of true men- who could possibly leave their homes. I hesitated not a moment in tendering my services- my life in *defence* of that flag which has waved so long and gloriously over our common country. I have every confidence that the justice of our cause, and the *unanimity* of feeling throughout the North will bring us a speedy victory, in fact the South will eat themselves out of house and home.[2]

In the First Rhode Island, Arnold was detached to the regiment's carbineer company, armed with Burnside carbines. One eyewitness wrote that Arnold performed with "intrepidity and coolness" on the skirmish line at Bull Run. He was mustered out with the First Rhode Island on August 2, 1861.[3]

Arnold spent several months at home in Providence, but by the fall of 1861, he was ready to return to field service. Arnold

---

[1] Augustus Woodbury, *A Narrative of the Campaign of the First Rhode Island Regiment, in the Spring and Summer of 1861.* (Providence: Sidney S. Rider, 1862), 189: 224. Job Arnold to James Shaw, June 23, 1861, courtesy of Meredith Sweet.
[2] Job Arnold to James Shaw, May 15, 1861, courtesy of Meredith Sweet.
[3] Hopkins, *Seventh Rhode Island,* 319-320.

received his commission as captain of Company E, Fifth Rhode Island Battalion, a small unit of five companies raised explicitly for the Burnside Coastal Expedition on December 6, 1861. The regiment was later renamed the Fifth Rhode Island Heavy Artillery.[4]

As a member of the Fifth Rhode Island, attached to the Burnside Expedition, Arnold fought at Roanoke, New Bern, and the Siege of Fort Macon in March-April 1862. Arnold passed the time between battles drawing sketches of the countryside, fishing for trout as well as hunting plovers, a type of shore bird which he considered "not bad for food." The Fifth Rhode Island was heavily engaged at New Bern. He wrote about the enemy he was facing, "If their grand army is composed of such material as the army captured on Roanoke they will stand no kind of chance in the open field for such a set of cutthroats I never saw together before. Everyone was armed with a knife as long as your arm of the rudest kind." After the victory at Fort Macon, the Fifth garrisoned the citadel, as Arnold had his first interactions with local slaves whom he considered "intelligent and jolly."

With the resignation of the Fifth's commander in August 1862, Arnold found himself the ranking captain and took command of the battalion, then in the process of expanding to ten companies. Arnold instrumented a radical training program to prepare the new regiment for future service, ordering constant inspections and close order drill. He got his chance to prove the value of this education in December 1862, leading the Fifth in the Goldsboro Raid where they saw combat at Rawle's Mills, Kinston, Whitehall, and Goldsboro. On January 7, 1863, Arnold was commissioned lieutenant colonel of the Fifth for "gallant services."[5]

---

[4] John K. Burlingame, *History of the Fifth Regiment of Rhode Island Heavy Artillery, During Three Years and a Half of Service in North Carolina, January 1862-June 1865*. (Providence: Snow & Farnum, 1892), 299.
[5] Burlingame, *Fifth Rhode Island,* 15-100. Job Arnold to James Shaw, February 15, 1862, April 8, 1862, and April 11, 1862, courtesy of Meredith Sweet.

Arnold's tenure as the commander of the Fifth Rhode Island was short lived, on March 2, 1863 he was transferred to the Seventh Rhode Island Volunteers, attached to the Ninth Corps, and then on its way to duty in Kentucky. The Seventh suffered significant losses at Fredericksburg, including the deaths of both the lieutenant colonel and the major, along with forty-six other members of the regiment. Prior to setting out to Kentucky, the Seventh's new lieutenant colonel, George E. Church had been promoted to colonel of the Eleventh Rhode Island. Instead of promoting Major Thomas Tobey, whom Colonel Bliss considered "young and of not much experience, a brave soldier," Arnold was transferred to the Seventh. Before leaving North Carolina, he was presented with a sash and field glasses by the members of the Fifth Rhode Island, as well as given an elaborate party by the officers of the regiment.[6]

Arnold, a well-known combat veteran was welcomed into the regiment over the hated Lieutenant Colonel Church. Drummer William Palmer Hopkins recorded, "A favorable impression is entertained concerning him, as it is known he was well liked by his comrades in North Carolina." The promotion was not universally welcome by the officers of the Seventh, who felt that an outsider should not have been commissioned into the regiment. Writing to recently resigned Captain David Kenyon, then at home in Richmond, Rhode Island, Lieutenant Edwin L. Hunt wrote. "Job Arnold of the 5th Battalion is Lieut. Col. of the 7th Ha! Ha! I reckon that some scorn looks are around the camp to night. I should not be surprised if some of the officers come home on the strength of it." Contrary to Hunt's predictions, no Seventh Rhode Island officer resigned over the promotion of Arnold, and in time he came to be widely respected among the officer corps of the regiment. Unfortunately for Arnold, he joined the Seventh Rhode Island for the Mississippi Campaign. The Seventh and the Ninth Corps were sent as reinforcements to Vicksburg in June 1863. Composed largely of New Englanders, the men of the Ninth Corps

---

[6] Regimental Descriptive Book, Seventh Rhode Island Volunteers, Rhode Island State Archives. Zenas R. Bliss to William Sprague, December 30, 1862, Rhode Island State Archives. Hopkins, *Seventh Rhode Island,* 320-321.

suffered terribly to the tropical diseases such as malaria, yellow fever, Yazoo Fever, typhoid, and dysentery they encountered in Mississippi.[7]

After the surrender, the regiment took part in the Siege of Jackson in mid-July, before embarking back up the Mississippi River in August. Only seventy-eight members of the Seventh were able to perform duty when the regiment arrived back in Cincinnati on August 20, 1863. Arnold contracted malaria during the two-month sojourn in Mississippi and his health was ruined. Despite being continually ill, Arnold was "untiring in his endeavors to develop, to the utmost, gentlemanly and soldierly habits in all under his command." He attempted to stay with the regiment, but could barely mount a horse. In October 1863, Arnold was stricken with dysentery "which rendered him unfit for duty." Eventually with his health continuing to decline, he was sent back to Providence on recruiting duty. Lieutenant Colonel Arnold never returned to service in the Seventh Rhode Island. Dr. Sprague of the Seventh wrote, "In my opinion his sickness was brought on by the severe hardship + exposure incidental to the Mississippi Campaign."[8]

Unable to perform any more duty with the Seventh, Arnold received a surgeon's certificate and went home to Providence. Like many members of the regiment, he returned home, severely ill with malaria and dysentery from his service in the "death swamps" around Vicksburg. He did not leave his room for five months, and required constant medical care. Arnold had hoped to rejoin the Seventh for the Overland Campaign of 1864,

---

[7] Hopkins, *Seventh Rhode Island,* 73. Edwin L. Hunt to David R. Kenyon, March 7, 1863, author's collection.
[8] Albert G. Sprague to "Captain Woodward," October 30, 1863, James Harris Papers, Rhode Island Historical Society, Providence, RI. Hopkins, *Seventh Rhode Island,* 135. Albert Sprague, Surgeon's Certificate for Job Arnold, October 16, 1864, courtesy of Meredith Sweet.

but instead was discharged for disability from the service on May 28, 1864.[9]

Arnold attempted to reenter the jewelry business, but his health prevented him from completing the fine detail required of the work. He married Anna Maria Angell on June 16, 1864 and had two children. Unable to work, he filed for a pension in October 1864 and began to collect thirty dollars per month. He was active in veteran's affairs, and joined Rodman Post #12, Grand Army of the Republic in 1868. Arnold enjoyed married life to Anna in Providence. He particularly enjoyed being a father, attending musical events, and frequently entertaining comrades from the Fifth Rhode Island at his home; Arnold's wife felt that he always regretted his decision leaving the Fifth Rhode Island for the Seventh as Arnold had "raised it to what it was."

Arnold's health continued to decline. One Seventh Rhode Island veteran wrote, "Being of a delicate organization, the disease which had fastened itself upon him could not be shaken off." Eventually Arnold "gradually wasted away." Arnold's wife Maria and his best friend James Shaw remained by his side to the end. In her meticulously kept journal of her married life, Maria recorded:

On Christmas morning the sun rose gloriously. My dear soldier kept his bed for the <u>first time.</u> I could not wish him a Merry Christmas knowing how he was but as we kissed each other I told him I prayed that it might be a peaceful one and I think it was so. Father and Mother came over bringing evergreen wreaths for him and a <u>great</u> doll for Mamie which she in her great delight ran up to show "papa". Gen. Shaw stood by the bed and took it from her after she had made it "tiss papa" on both cheeks. Mamie looked happy and bright with her new outfit on and Job seemed pleased with her and praised dolly smiling feebly, and kissing <u>"his little girl"</u> as he called her. Mamie went with grandpa and grandma to the <u>Mansion House</u> to stay all day. Albert called on the morning to see and say us "good-bye." He desired me to tell Job how gladly

---

[9] Medical Report of Job Arnold, June 4, 1864, courtesy of Meredith Sweet. Job Arnold, Pension and Service File, National Archives. Hopkins, *Seventh Rhode Island,* 322.

he would do, for Mamie and me. In the evening Mrs. Talbot came and staid through the night. Sunday morning found Job, as his Doct. had given warning, he was weaker than ever. Gen Shaw helped me to get him in bed to take his dinner. He did not rest his feet on the floor as on the previous day. Saturday night Mrs. Hawkins staid with me. Job talked less than on the previous night. He has never been aware of my having watchers, except when my sister has been here – I simply need some one to sleep with Mamie to take care of her if she wakes. On Monday Mr. Woodbury called – he stood beside the bed and spoke to Job of the noble life he had spent here which would never be forgotten. "You will not go from us," he said, "we shall always keep you with us in thought. Such men can never leave us." Then he said, "Shall I offer a prayer?" my brave soldier moved his head in assent and folded his hands on his breast. I clasping my own over them and together we three offered the prayer so sacred. I told Mr. Woodbury after the prayer, I had always wanted to be <u>alone</u> with my husband and him when that prayer was sent up. I cannot forget the great tear that stood from his cheek as he left us. My husband asked him in his courteous way, "Come again" yet knowing he would scarcely be present in life.

I could only sorrow for the loss of the love and compassion, that I had no sins of his to suffer for. His life had been <u>good and brave,</u> and I knew how he needed rest from pain.

At four o'clock Tuesday morning I went in to my husband's room and sat by his bed. When I leaned over and kissed him he took my hand and kissed me in return. I said, "Job you do love me don't you?" He replied <u>"Yes indeed I do."</u> Then I said, "Kiss me once more" and he did so saying, "<u>Now the Doct. is coming. I must go with him.</u> You had better go. I do not like this nurse." (for the first time we had a man come in at 12 in the evening, it being necessary to lift my husband at times) "he stares at me so – send him away – I am going home with the Doctor." I saw how weak his mind and body were and ran quickly into the neighboring house to call Gen. Shaw. Very early our good Doctor came and before eight of the evening of the following day, there was rest for the dear brave soldier whose work was done. There were dear friends present before he passed away to whom he spoke rationally. One bent over and said some kind words in so low a tone I could not hear them.

They were alone –

Last of all he said once, "Where is Mamie?" and when she was brought in by Gen. Shaw, he said "This is my little girl" and she said, "Mamie loves papa" and they kissed each other.

After he had remained some time quiet, I said "Are you in pain?" "Pain in the right lung." Then when I said again, "Do you know me?" he said "Yes, now don't wake me any more." And so the soldier passed away with all my love for him I could thank God for giving him rest at last.

Lieutenant Colonel Job Arnold died of disease contracted in the service on December 28, 1869. He was the final Rhode Islander to perish from the effects of the Vicksburg Campaign.[10]

The local *Providence Journal,* as well as his pension records made it clear that Arnold died as a direct result of his service with the Seventh Rhode Island in Mississippi. In 1871, his name was inscribed on the Soldiers and Sailors Monument in Providence.[11]

Captain William W. Douglas of the Fifth Rhode Island eulogized his former commander:

He was a soldier of perfect courage and endurance, an officer whose rare judgement made him a leader among

---

[10] Arnold, Pension File. Anna Maria Arnold "Journal 1867-1869 First Years in the Life of Mary Angell Arnold and Last Days in the Life of Lt. Col. Job Arnold," courtesy of Meredith Sweet. Resolutions to family of Job Arnold, December 30, 1869, courtesy of Meredith Sweet. Hopkins, *Seventh Rhode Island,* 322.

[11] *Providence Journal,* December 29, 1869. *Proceedings at the Dedication of the Soldiers and Sailors Monument in Providence.* (Providence: A. Crawford Greene, 1871), 54.

his compeers, whose firmness and gentleness won the respect and affection of his subordinates, and whose military skill and promptness secured the confidence of his commanders, a patriot who willingly accepted a lingering and painful death as the result of his services to his country; a friend who was ever regardless of self in the service of those he love, a man of cheerful temper, amiable heart, and unsullied purity of life.[12]

Lieutenant Colonel Job Arnold was laid to rest in North Burial Ground, in Providence. A veteran of three Rhode Island regiments, his widow Anna had inscribed upon his tombstone, "Lieut Col 7 Reg R-I-V."

---

[12] Hopkins, *Seventh Rhode Island,* 322.

Chapter Six:

"Martyrs to the Cause of Liberty:"

The Hopkinton Boys of the Fighting Fourth

The Civil War soldiers from Hopkinton left behind arguably the finest written record of any Rhode Island community during the conflict, as told through the scores of letters they wrote home. The town was then, as now, a quiet, close knit community. It is hard to imagine that 204 men from Hopkinton served in the Civil War, going to the front in every one of the Rhode Island's Civil War regiments. One out of every six Hopkinton recruits died in the service during the war; a casualty rate only exceeded by South Kingstown. Today only a small monument stands in Pine Grove Cemetery to honor their memory. The men from the villages of Ashaway, Locustville, Burdickville, Yawgoog, Rockville, Canonchet, and Hopkinton City are remembered by the words they left behind.[106]

In the fall of 1861, eleven men from Hopkinton, and the neighboring village of Potter Hill in Westerly joined the Fourth Rhode Island, the state's forgotten three-year infantry regiment,

---

[106] S.S. Griswold, *Historical Sketch of the Town of Hopkinton: From 1757 to 1876 comprising a period of 119 years.* (Hope Valley: L.W.A. Cole, 1877), 46-51. For two compilations of letters of Hopkinton soldiers refer to Kris VanDenBossche, ed. *"Pleas Excuse All Bad Writing:" A Documentary History of Rhode Island During the Civil War Era, 1854-1865.* (Peace Dale: Rhode Island Historical Document Transcription Project, 1993) and Kris VanDenBossche, *Write Soon and Give Me all the News: A Documentary History of Rhode Island During the Civil War Era.* (Peace Dale: Rhode Island Historical Document Transcription Project, 1993) There are also dozens of letters from Hopkinton soldiers at the Rhode Island Historical Society and in private collections.

largely overshadowed by the actions of the Second and Seventh Rhode Island Volunteers. Raised primarily in Newport and Providence Counties, the men from Hopkinton were given the moniker of "The South County Boys" by their comrades from Chepachet, where most of Company D was recruited.[107]

Organized after the Union defeat at Bull Run in the late summer of 1861, the Fourth was nicknamed "The Fighting Fourth," by the *Providence Journal.* Originally commanded by Isaac Peace Rodman (who as a general died at Antietam), the Fourth was sent to North Carolina in the spring of 1862, and played a prominent role in the Battles of Roanoke, New Bern and Fort Macon; among the treasured relics of the Rhode Island National Guard is a Confederate flag the Fourth captured at New Bern. After a near mutiny in the summer of 1862 over who was to command the regiment, the unit formed the extreme left flank of the Army of the Potomac at the Battle of Antietam. Marching blindly into a cornfield, the Fourth was ambushed by an entire Confederate brigade. Alone, and unsupported, the Fourth retreated after suffering fifty percent casualties. In December 1862, the Fourth fought at Fredericksburg, losing their commander, Lieutenant Colonel Joseph B. Curtis. In the spring of 1863, the regiment was transferred to Suffolk, Virginia, spending much of the next year on guard duty.

Assigned to guard Confederate prisoners in Maryland in the winter of 1864, the Fourth missed out on the carnage in the spring of 1864 as part of Grant's Overland Campaign. The Fighting Fourth returned to the Army of the Potomac in July of 1864 in time for the Siege of Petersburg. They were in the front line during the July 30, 1864 Battle of the Crater, and again suffered heavily. On September 30, 1864, the Fourth fought in one

---

[107] *Narragansett Weekly, March 12, 1863. Providence Evening Press,* Sept. 1-9, 1861.George B. Carpenter, "War and Other Reminiscences," Edited by Kris VanDenBossche. *Rhode Island History,* Vol. 47, No. 4, November 1989, 118-119. This is a transcribed version of Carpenter's superb post-war memoirs of his service in the Fourth Rhode Island. The original typescript is located in the Local History Room of the Westerly Memorial Library.

more battle at Poplar Spring Church, Virginia; three men died hours before they were supposed to return to Rhode Island. When the rest of the regiment went home, 226 men who had reenlisted were transferred to the Seventh Rhode Island in November 1864, thus ending the history of this proud unit. The consolidation with the Seventh Rhode Island was a bitter end to the history of the Fourth. Corporal George H. Allen proudly wrote, "We were *once* and *always* the Fourth Rhode Island Regiment." The Hopkinton Boys were part of all of this action.[108]

Besides forming a unique part of a regiment recruited in northern Rhode Island, two other factors set the Hopkinton Boys apart. Most were members of the Seventh Day Baptist Church. Believing that the true Sabbath was on a Saturday, instead of a Sunday further set these men apart as having a unique war time experience in the ranks of the Fighting Fourth.[109]

In addition, nine of the eleven went to the Hopkinton Academy in Ashaway, a traditional New England lyceum. Tuition was three to six dollars per a semester, depending on the courses selected. The Academy brought instruction in the arts, sciences, and music to many who previously only had access to a rudimentary education at the local district school. Many of the classes there were taught by Joseph W. Morton, a Seventh Day Baptist minister who himself went to war as a lieutenant in the Seventh Rhode Island in the fall of 1862. At the academy, the students were taught heavily in the language arts; this was reflected in the excellent letters these men left behind chronicling their time in the service during the Civil War. Despite the excellent education they were receiving, most of the older students

---

[108] *Providence Journal,* March 25-April 4, 1862. Carpenter, "War and Other Reminiscences," 115-147. For a complete history of the Fourth, refer to George H. Allen, *Forty-Six Months with the Fourth Rhode Island Volunteers in the War of 1861-1865, Comprising a History of its Marches, Battles, and Camp Life.* (Providence: J.A & R.A. Reid), 1887.
[109] Civil War military service records, First, Second, and Third Seventh Day Baptist Churches of Hopkinton, Rhode Island, Seventh Day Baptist Historical Society, Janesville, WI.

could not resist the call to arms when they discovered that another regiment was being called for from Rhode Island.

In late September 1861, with the war raging, the eleven Hopkinton men went to Providence to volunteer. Although they enlisted on different days, most found their way into Company D, thus retaining the same friendships and bonds they had developed in school. Most of the other men in Company D, which was largely recruited in Chepachet, were farmers and mill laborers. The combination of religion and education further set apart the experiences of the men from Hopkinton.[110]

Although these men all came from the same corner of south-west Rhode Island, news of their service and sacrifice was hardly covered in the local *Narragansett Weekly,* a newspaper in Westerly that covered the beat in Stonington, Hopkinton, Richmond, Charlestown, and Westerly. In the March 12, 1863 edition of the *Narragansett Weekly,* Horace Stillman, wrote a very moving letter that tells of the effect of a year and a half of war on the men from this corner of Rhode Island.

Fourth Rhode Island Regiment

The Hopkinton Boys

It is now seventeen months since nine of my comrades and myself left our homes, and enlisted in the 4th R.I. Regiment, which was being formed at Providence. There we remained for nearly three weeks, until the regiment was full, when we removed to Washington, where we were placed in General Casey's Division,[111] General Howard's[112] Brigade, and were stationed

---

[110] Carpenter, "War and Other Reminiscences," 110-111.
VanDenBossche, *Pleas Excuse,* 23-26. William P. Hopkins, *The Seventh Regiment Rhode Island Volunteers in the Civil War, 1862-1865.* (Providence: Snow and Farnum, 1903), 368-370. Company D, Fourth R.I. Descriptive Book.
[111] Major General Silas Casey, 1807-1882, was a native of North Kingstown and commanded Union troop around Washington during the

about six miles from Washington near Bladensburg, Md, where we remained but a short time, and then removed into Virginia near Alexandria, and were placed in Sumner's Division.

About this time, Gen. Burnside's expedition was being fitted out to go to North Carolina, and it was rumored around camp, that our regiment was to go with him; but we let it pass, as we do all camp stories, without placing any reliance upon it, until the order came, at midnight after New Year's Day for us to strike tents at three o'clock, and get ready to go to Annapolis, Md, and to join the expedition.

We accordingly got ready, marched to Washington, and took the cars to Annapolis, where we pitched tents, and remained about a week; when we entered the transports that afterwards bore us to our place of destination. We remained on board of the vessels for more than a month, at Hatteras Inlet, where we were buffeted about by the rough sea; and when the day arrived for us to start for the enemy, we were much delighted.

As you are aware, our first engagement with the enemy was upon Roanoke Island, where our gun boats broke the stillness of the day, filling the air with an almost unbroken sound, like the roaring of heavy thunder, when the cloud is passing directly overhead; while the white smoke that always attends the bursting of a shell, became more and more dense, until the works of the enemy were hid from our view. Yet we could plainly see the flash of our guns that were silencing one after another of the guns of the enemy, until they were driven from the three forts that were

---

war. He wrote the standard Union Infantry tactics manual known as Casey's Tactics." He is buried on the Casey Farm in North Kingstown. Mark M. Boatner III, *The Civil War Dictionary.* (New York: David McKay, 1988), 131.

[112] Major General Oliver Otis Howard, 1830-1909, was a native of Maine. He commanded Union troops in the eastern and western theaters during the war. After the war, Howard was in command of the Freedmen's Bureau, and founded Howard University. He is buried in Burlington, Vermont. Boatner, *Civil War Dictionary,* 413-414.

intended to command the sound, and effectually prevent the landing of our troops.

We landed without being molested; but there was still a work to do, that must be accomplished by infantry alone, for when the rebels were compelled to abandon their works in front, they fell back into a masked battery in the swamp, about the distance of a mile from shore, and there concealed themselves prepared for battle, and awaited the approach of the infantry. The 1st Brigade was the first to enter the conflict; they engaged the rebels for about two hours, and then were relieved by the 2d Brigade, which gave them battle about the same length of time as the 1st. By that time, General Burnside had become so familiar with their position as to enable him to make a flank movement. So our regiment was ordered to move around to the left, and one of the Massachusetts regiments, and the 9th New York was to make a charge in front.[113] This movement was effectually accomplished, but with great difficulty, for we had to wade through mud and water that was more than three feet deep, and the rebels discovered out movement, and discharged their pieces that were loaded with grape and canister at us, but the contents went over our heads, and none of our boys in the 4th R.I. were injured. The whole force of the rebels was routed, and finally captured.

The next engagement that our regiment was in was at Newbern, NC where we lost about fifty men in killed and wounded.[114] Two of them were among the nine whom I mentioned

---

[113] The Ninth New York was also known as "Hawkins' Zouaves," and was commanded by Rush C. Hawkins, who married into the Brown Family of Providence. Today his war relics and art collection reside at the Ann Mary Brown Memorial at Brown University, which is a must visit site for history lovers. Matthew J. Graham, *The Ninth Regiment New York Volunteers (Hawkins' Zouaves).* (New York: E.P. Cory, 1900), 1-23

[114] At New Bern, seventeen members of the Fourth Rhode Island were killed or mortally wounded, an additional fourteen were wounded in some form. Fourth Rhode Island Descriptive Books.

in the commencement as having volunteered at the time of my enlistment. One was Davis Crandall of Rockville.[115] He was almost instantly killed, while our regiment was charging a rifle pit, where the enemy were firmly posted. His conduct was such as to command the respect and admiration of all of his company. His true and manly courage is certainly deserving of the highest praise. The other that I mentioned was Edwin Gavitt of Ashaway. He, although not killed upon the field, received a wound that proved fatal, though at first it was believed that he would recover. He, like his comrades, was brave and true and highly esteemed by all who knew him. He suffered much, but bore it all with a patience that showed his resignation to the will of his Creator.[116]

Time passed on, and a few weeks brought us upon Bogue Island, in front of Fort Macon, which at that time was held by the rebels, and garrisoned by about five hundred men. It was constructed very strong upon the south and east sides, and we calculated principally as a defense against naval attacks; so, but our gaining its rear, we had only to construct batteries of sand, in order, if need be, to demolish it. These batteries we constructed in the night, where our men could not conceal themselves behind

---

[115] Davis Crandall was a twenty-year-old single farm who resided in Rockville. He enlisted September 27, 1861 and was killed in action at New Bern, North Carolina on March 14, 1862. He is buried in Rockville Cemetery, Hopkinton Historical Cemetery # 6. Company D, Fourth Rhode Island Volunteers, Descriptive Book, R.I. State Archives. Gayle E. Waite and Lorraine Tarket-Arruda, *Hopkinton, Rhode Island Historical Cemeteries.* (Baltimore: Gateway Press, 1998), NP, entry HP #6. Crandall's letters are contained in VanDenBossche, *Pleas Excuse All Bad Writing,* 23-57,

[116] Edwin Dallas Gavitt was a single eighteen-year-old student from Ashaway when he enlisted September 25, 1861. He was shot in the leg at New Bern and sent to a hospital in New York to recover. The leg was amputated, and the wound proved fatal; he died on June 16, 1862. Gavitt's remains were brought back to Rhode Island and interred in Oak Grove Cemetery in Ashaway. Company D, Fourth Rhode Island Volunteers, Descriptive Book. Waite and Tarket Arruda, *Hopkinton Cemeteries,* entry for HP # 18.

sand banks from the sight of the secesh so as to work in the day. When our men showed their heads above the banks, they would open fire upon us from the fort, and their shells burst all around us; but none of us were injured while the works were being constructed. The fort was finally taken, after about eight hours fight; but, as I said before, our regiment sustained no loss.

We left North Carolina with Burnside, when a command was assigned to him in the Army of the Potomac; our regiment was in the battle of South Mountain, Md, but sustained no lost there. A few days more brought on the Battle of Antietam, and there the 4th R.I., suffered severely as did most of the regiments that were engaged; many brave men were instantly laid prostrate in death's cold embrace, while other were suffering severely from the effects of wounds.[117] Among the first that fell was Corporal Benjamin Burdick of Rockville[118], one of the nine that I mentioned in the commencement. He was struck by a minie ball, that passed through his chest. While Henry Saunders, another of our number was assisting in carrying him from the field, before life was extinct, he also received a fatal wound. Mr. Burdick lived only a few moments, but before he died he took some treasures from his pocket, that were gifts of remembrance from his friends at Rockville, and requested them to be sent to his home, and he soon passed away.

---

[117] By day's end on September 17, 1862, the Fourth Rhode Island Volunteers lost roughly thirty dead, eighty wounded, and five captured at Antietam. This was fifty percent of the roughly 220 men the regiment brought into combat that day. The Fourth's losses at Antietam are second only to the heavy casualties the Seventh Rhode Island suffered three months later at Fredericksburg. Fourth Rhode Island Volunteers, Casualty Returns and Descriptive Books, Rhode Island State Archives.

[118] Corporal Benjamin Franklin Burdick, a single, twenty-year-old farmer from Rockville was killed at Antietam. A cenotaph for Burdick exists in the Rockville Cemetery. He is actually buried in the Rhode Island plot at the Antietam National Cemetery. Waite and Tarket Arruda, *Hopkinton Cemeteries,* entry for HP #6. Company D, Fourth Rhode Island Volunteers, Descriptive Book. Interment Records, Antietam National Cemetery, Sharpsburg, Maryland.

He, like his comrades who had gone before him, had won the respect of all his company, as well as of all who knew him. As a soldier, he was faithful, brave, and true, and did all in his power for the welfare of our country, and well may our nation mourn the loss of such devoted patriots. Mr. Saunders, of Potter Hill, received a wound that at first was deemed curable by most of us; but as time passed on he grew worse instead of improving, and in a few weeks passed away.[119] He, too, was a faithful friend and a true supporter of the Union cause, and his loss was deeply felt by his comrades in arms, as well as by his friends, at home. Another of our number has just returned to the regiment from Richmond, where he has been a prisoner.[120] The rest of us have escaped thus far unharmed.

H. Stillman
Co. I 4th R.I.V.[121]

Newport News, Va, March 4th 1863.

Of the eleven men who served in the Hopkinton contingent of the Fourth Rhode Island, only four survived the war unscathed. Four men were killed in action, and another, Sergeant

---

[119] Henry Freeman Saunders was a single, twenty-year-old laborer from Ashaway and enlisted October 3, 1861. According to Sergeant George B. Carpenter who was present at Antietam, Saunders was shot in the shoulder, the bullet passing into his chest as he tried to drag the severely wounded Benjamin Burdick off the field. He died of his wounds at a field hospital near Sharpsburg, Maryland on October 25, 1862. He is buried in Oak Grove Cemetery in Ashaway. Company D, Fourth Rhode Island Volunteers, Descriptive Book. Waite and Tarket Arruda, *Hopkinton Cemeteries,* entry for HP # 18. Carpenter, "Days and Events," 131-132.

[120] William A. Weeks, a single twenty-two-year-old farmer from Rockville was captured in action at Antietam. Released from prison, he mustered out with the regiment on October 15, 1864. Company K, Fourth Rhode Island Volunteers, Descriptive Book.

[121] Despite volunteering from Hopkinton, Horace Stillman was assigned to Company I, recruited out of Pawtucket. He was a single farmer, and enlisted on September 20, 1861. He was discharged for disability on June 1, 1864 at Portsmouth Grove Hospital. Company I, Fourth Rhode Island Volunteers, Descriptive Book.

George B. Carpenter lost his right arm at the Battle of the Crater. Only four men were well enough to muster out with the regiment and return home in October of 1864.[122]

Private Davis Crandall was the first Hopkinton soldier to die in the Civil War. Unlike many other men from the town who perished, his family was able to bring his remains back home to be buried in Rockville. On April 2, 1862, the Hopkinton Town Council unanimously passed a touching resolution in honor of Crandall:

> Whereas, Davis Crandall, a young man and citizen of this town, did respond promptly to the call of his country; leaving home and friends to defend the interests we hold so dear, and having gained the confidence of his officers and comrades, and suffered much in camp has fallen a martyr to the cause of liberty, being killed at Newbern, N.C. March 14th, 1862, while charging the enemy, therefore:
>
> Resolved, that we deem it our duty to commend the noble impulse which led him to make this sacrifice for freedom, and that we extend to the afflicted family of which he was a member, our warmest sympathies with the kind assurance that we appreciate the noble conduct of this dutiful son.[123]

For the survivors, it became a part of their life to remember their comrades who died in the war. On the first Decoration Day, Civil War veterans from Westerly marched to Oak Grove Cemetery in Ashaway and placed fresh flowers on the graves of Edwin Dallas Gavitt and Henry Freeman Saunders. Samuel and Eliza Crandall mourned the loss of their son Davis who fell at New Bern. The brief epitaph they chose for their son is a fitting memorial to the

---

[122] Fourth Rhode Island Volunteers, Descriptive Books and Regimental Casualty Returns, Rhode Island State Archives.
[123] Griswold, *Sketch of Hopkinton,* 47-48.

Hopkinton Boys of the forgotten Fighting Fourth Rhode Island Volunteers: "For My Country"[124]

---

[124] *Narragansett Weekly,* June 3, 1868. Records of Budlong Post #18, Department of Rhode Island, Grand Army of the Republic, Westerly Memorial Library, Archives, Westerly, Rhode Island.

83

Chapter Seven:

"I have never heard of him since:"

The case of James A. Matteson

In the early morning hours of October 19, 1864 along the banks of Cedar Creek, just south of Middletown, Virginia, a large Confederate army under the command of General Jubal Early prepared to strike the sleeping Union forces in their encampment. As the rebel yell and the crack of musketry filled the dawn air, thousands of Union soldiers ran for their lives. Into the mealy rode Colonel Charles H. Tompkins of Providence. A thirty-year-old combat veteran of many bloody battles, and the commander of the First Rhode Island Light Artillery Regiment, Tompkins also led the Sixth Corps Artillery Brigade. As a brigade of Alabamians bore down in front of him, he quickly spotted Lieutenant Jacob Lamb and Captain George W. Adams, commanding Battery C and Battery G, First Rhode Island Light Artillery respectively and ordered them to hold their position at all costs until reinforcements could arrive.[1]

Tompkins dismounted from his horse to help Battery G in its withdrawal, but was quickly shot in the arm and went to the rear. Two of the prized Parrott rifles of Battery C had already fallen to the enemy, Lieutenant Lamb would not let the other two meet the same fate. With nearly a third of his men down, he gave the order for double canister, which effectively turned the cannon into the world's largest shotgun, to be fired at the enemy. A fellow

---

[1] John R. Bartlett, *Memoirs of Rhode Island Officers who were engaged in the service of their Country during the Great Rebellion of the South.* (Providence: S.S. Rider & Brother, 1867), 381-382. James A. Barber, Diary entry for October 19, 1864, John Hay Library, Brown University, Providence, RI.

soldier watching on recalled, "Lamb's C 1st Rhode Island got into a hot place and was made the subject of a rough and tumble fight." In an instant the Alabamians were mowed down into a pink mist in front of the bedazzled Rhode Islanders. Pulling their guns out of a slight depression, the men from the smallest state received a most welcome surprise as the Old Vermont Brigade launched a desperate counterattack to save the cannons. The Rhode Islanders were finally safe, but across the field lay the carnage of combat and dozens of dead and wounded Rhode Islanders, Alabamians, and Vermonters. Among the Rhode Islanders who would never be seen again was James A. Matteson of Scituate. [2]

The service and pension files contained within the National Archives contain some of the best records for the study of Rhode Island's Civil War soldiers. Often filled with details of injuries and sickness, the struggle to obtain a pension after the war, as well as pertinent genealogical information, these records are a treasure. For genealogists they provide important information regarding family dynamics, where people moved after the war, and sometimes contain the actual letters of the soldiers themselves that family members sent to Washington in a desperate attempt to get a pension after their loved one failed to return home. Importantly they are now being studied by scholars to reveal that the true cost of the Civil War was much higher than previously thought, nearly 750,000. [3]

The subject of this study, James A. Matteson (sometimes referred to as Maddison, Mathewson, or Mattison) in the army records was born on January 4, 1843 in Scituate, Rhode Island. He was the son of Rhoda and Henry Matteson, who was a farmer. In total, the Matteson family consisted of the parents and seven children, born between 1839 and 1856. James' early life would have been uneventful, working on the family's small farm and attending class in the winter. James' life continued unabated until

---

[2] Augustus C. Buell, *"The Cannoneer." Recollections of Service in the Army of the Potomac.* (Washington, D.C.: National Tribune, 1890), 303-308. James A. Matteson, Service File, National Archives, Washington, DC.

[3] *New York Times,* April 2, 2012.

1861, when like many other young men, he felt the need to enlist to preserve the Union. He was seventeen years old at the time, and would have needed parental permission to enlist, which was granted by Henry and Rhoda as he promised to send his entire pay home.[4]

Even twenty years after the war, Rhoda remembered the last time she saw her son he was six feet, two inches tall. She recalled, "His hair was dark brown and the color of his eyes was a dark hazel." Matteson enlisted as a private in Battery C, First Rhode Island Light Artillery on August 25, 1865. Unfortunately, none of his wartime letters are known to survive. Recruited from throughout the state, Battery C was composed largely of men from Providence, but also included smaller detachments from South County, as well as the Pawtucket area. The unit went south in August 1861 and was assigned to the Washington area.[5]

After a winter of training, the battery, under the command of future Rhode Island historian Captain William B. Weeden was assigned to the Fifth Corps of the Army of the Potomac. With the Fifth Corps, Battery C went on to see heavy combat on the Virginia Peninsula, where on June 27, 1862 they were overrun by a brigade of Texans. Several days later, five men were killed in a friendly fire incident at Malvern Hill. The unit was also engaged at Antietam, Fredericksburg, and Chancellorsville. In the late spring of 1863, Battery C was transferred to the Sixth Corps, and the men followed the corps to Gettysburg, but were not heavily engaged. Further combat came in the spring of 1864 at the Wilderness, Spotsylvania Court House, Cold Harbor, and Petersburg.

---

[4] Scituate, Rhode Island, Birth, Marriage, and Death Records, 1825-1875, Town Clerk's Office, Scituate, RI. Rhoda Matteson, Description of Family in support of pension, December 28, 1882, James A. Matteson Pension File, National Archives. Rhode Island did not utilize single enlistment papers until 1862, when the Seventh Rhode Island Volunteers were recruited. Men enlisted in 1861 filled out their records in large muster books, which are now in the custody of the Rhode Island State Archives.

[5] Rhoda Matteson, Claimant's Testimony, December 28, 1882, Matteson Pension File.

Transferred to the Shenandoah Valley in August 1864, the original members of the battery who had not reenlisted were sent home for muster out. Reduced to fewer than 90 men from an authorized strength of 150, the remaining soldiers fought at the Battle of Opequon on September 19, and three days later followed up the victory at Fisher's Hill. Private James A. Matteson remarkably survived all these engagements unscathed until his luck ran out at Cedar Creek on October 19, 1864.[6]

At some point during the early morning melee for the guns, Private Matteson was shot in the head by an Alabama soldier. As his comrades ran for their lives, they had no choice but to abandon the wounded as they rushed to try to save their cannon and reform a line to stop the Confederate assault. The Confederates captured several wounded Rhode Island soldiers, but Private Matteson was not among them. To complicate the matters of his case, soon after the battle, Battery C and Battery G were consolidated into a single unit, called Battery G. On the final muster roll of Battery C, Matteson is listed as "Absent in Hospital Wounded." He continued to be listed as wounded, in the hospital until the final muster out roll of Battery G, dated June 24, 1865 when he was reported "Was in hospital of Artillery Brigade 6th A.C. at the battle of Cedar Creek Va, October 19, 1865 with fractured cranial. Investigation fails to elicit further investigation." Although carried on the muster rolls as being in the hospital

---

[6] Unfortunately, Battery C, First Rhode Island Light Artillery was one of the three Rhode Island units (the others being Battery G and the Third Rhode Island Cavalry) that never published a regimental history. The most pertinent sources for published regimental information are Edwin Winchester Stone, *Rhode Island in the Rebellion*. (Providence: G.H. Whitney, 1865). Stone was a private in the battery and these letters were published in the *Providence Journal*. In addition, Stone wrote a brief sketch of the battery for the *Revised Register of Rhode Island Volunteers*. Furthermore, the letters of Lieutenant Frederic M. Sackett at the Rhode Island Historical Society are very important for the period through Chancellorsville, where he was wounded.

wounded, it was clear that no one in either Battery C or Battery G ever saw James A. Matteson alive again.[7]

Back in Scituate the news arrived one day that Private Matteson was missing in action, and presumed dead. In December of 1863, Matteson had reenlisted as a veteran volunteer, earning a five-hundred-dollar bonus, and a thirty-day furlough home. The money, along with any back pay would have been sent to the family in Scituate. It is clear from the army records that James sent the majority of his pay home to his mother, and that his death represented a significant loss of income to the family.[8]

Henry Matteson, James' father owned about seventy acres in Scituate. The farm was valued at $600 dollars in 1864, but by 1878, as the population of Scituate began to expand, and land values soared, the property was now valued at $1,200, placing a severe tax burden on the struggling family as they got older and tried maintain the farm. Faced with losing the farm, in 1878 Henry mortgaged a portion of the farm to a neighbor for $200. Needing help to support herself, Rhoda filed for a Federal mother's pension on August 22, 1879. Under acts of Congress from 1862 and 1873, parents who were dependent upon their children for support, and died as a result of their war service could seek a pension. Little did Rhoda know of the difficulty she would have.[9]

Rhoda, as evidenced by her pension filings could not write, and left her "x" mark on her surviving documents. On August 6, 1879, at age fifty-nine she appeared before the Kent County Clerk of Court, Thomas M. Holden, and filed her pension. She declared that her son was James A. Matteson and that he "died at Middletown, Va from wounds on the 19 day of Oct 1864." She also swore that she had been dependent upon her son for support,

---

[7] Buell, *The Cannoneer,* 303-307. Muster Rolls of Battery C, First Rhode Island Light Artillery, September-December 1864 and Battery G, First Rhode Island Light Artillery, June 1865, National Archives.

[8] Veteran Volunteer Documents in Matteson Pension File.

[9] Daniel H. Remington, Affidavit in support of Rhoda Matteson, March 7, 1883, Matteson Pension File. Declaration for Mother's Pension, August 6, 1879, Matteson Pension File.

and that her husband Henry "is unable to fully support me on account of ill health." Two neighbors attested to these facts. Rhoda appointed an N.W. Fitzgerald, a pension agent from Washington, D.C. to represent her. She filled out the pension documents and sent them to Washington, hoping to receive the meager funds it would bring in.[10]

Rhoda's pension application was given claim number 250,167. Much as today, the government moved slowly on her application, and it took nearly two years to finally be reviewed by a clerk. On September 28, 1881, the War Department responded to a Pension Bureau request for information on James' death. They responded that he "Died October 19, 1864 at Middletown, Va from wounds as claimant states." The War Department stated that the information came from the muster rolls of Batteries C and G in their possession. Nominally, the statement from the War Department would be acceptable as final proof of a soldier's fate, however in the case of James Matteson; this would not be the case. The clerk from the Pension Bureau needed Rhoda to prove that her son actually died in combat at Cedar Creek, and that she was indigent as she stated on her declaration.[11]

Another inquiry to the War Department brought about a letter from Lieutenant Colonel Joseph J. Woodward that "James Maddison Priv. Co. C 1 R.I. Arty received a fracture of cranial bone at the battle of Middletown, Va Oct. 19, 1864." Like the War Department, Woodward based his report off of the "records of Battery C." A further inquiry revealed that Matteson had not been treated at a general hospital at Winchester, Virginia, Frederick, Maryland, or in Washington. Furthermore, Matteson had simply disappeared. In 1866, the government had removed many of the remains of Union soldiers who died in the northern Shenandoah Valley to the new Winchester National Cemetery; among them were a dozen Rhode Islanders. The body of James Matteson was

---

[10] Matteson, Declaration for Mother's Pension, August 6, 1879.
[11] William W. Dudley to War Department, September 28, 1881, Matteson Pension File.

90

never identified, and he was buried in an unmarked grave, presumably in the Winchester National Cemetery.[12]

While every indicator stated that Matteson had died shortly after being wounded at Cedar Creek, the Pension Bureau continued to seek further information that Matteson was not mortally wounded at Cedar Creek, and made it to a general hospital for treatment. A clerk wrote, "It is stated the soldier was placed in an ambulance the morning after the battle and carried to Winchester, Va and in a day or two was taken to a hospital in Winchester, Va and died." With much on the line, Rhoda began the painstaking process of gathering additional affidavits of support to help her case.[13]

On February 28, 1883, Andrew Burns and Charles McCarthy, two veterans who had served in Battery C with Matteson submitted an affidavit to the Pension Bureau in support of Rhoda. They stated:

> Matteson was *wounded* in the *head* in said action while in line of duty. He was thereby totally disabled, and fell into hands of the enemy. Later in the day our forces regained the field and Matteson was retaken by us. Both saw him after he was *retaken*, and saw that he was badly wounded in the *head* in *two places*. They never saw him afterwards. They heard the wounds spoken of so being fatal, and understood afterward that he was taken to some hospital and they subsequently heard the next day they think that he *died* of *his wounds*.[14]

---

[12] Joseph J. Woodward to Pension Bureau, March 23, 1882, Matteson Pension File. B.F. Pope to Adjutant General, U.S. Army, January 30, 1886. Information and Burial List for Winchester National Cemetery, http://www.cem.va.gov/CEM/cems/nchp/winchester.asp, accessed June 12, 2016.

[13] Notation returning letters to the Adjutant General for additional information, December 21, 1885, Matteson Pension File.

[14] Andrew Burns and Charles McCarthy, Affidavit, February 28, 1883, Matteson Pension File.

As stated by his comrades, Matteson died in a field hospital the day after he was wounded. With the horrible conditions facing the surgeons after the battle, they did not have time to keep accurate records, but rather to work long hours to try and save as many patients as possible. Matteson did not make it to a larger hospital, but rather was treated in the Artillery Brigade of the Sixth Corps field hospital on the field at Cedar Creek. The clerk at the Pension Office was even skeptical about the testimony of Burns and McCarthy and wrote to the War Department for information to confirm they were present with Battery C at Cedar Creek, which they were.[15]

While his comrades rallied to support Rhoda, she submitted her own statement that she remembered a physical description of her son, and added "I have never seen him since his re-enlistment on or about 1863, that I have been informed that he was wounded in battle and died at Hospital and I have never seen or heard of him since." When pressed to provide correspondence James had sent home, she replied "I further testify that few letters were *received* from the soldier and so far as I know they have all been destroyed or lost. Several other neighbors responded and wrote that "We knew of the enlistment of James A. Matteson and of his reported death and that we have *never seen or heard of him* since October 1864 and that we were informed that he was wounded in battle and died from the effects of his wounds." These affidavits appear to have been the tipping point, as Rhoda was finally able to prove that her son died in the Civil War.[16]

Having filed her original claim in 1879, by 1883 she was desperate for support. She wrote in a plea to the government for support:

---

[15] William W. Dudley to Adjutant General's Office, November 14, 1883 and Reply January 4, 1884, Matteson Pension File.

[16] Rhoda Matteson to Pension Bureau, December 28, 1882 and October 6, 1883, Matteson Pension File. Ezra K. Potter and Benoni C. Matteson, Affidavit in Support of Pension, March 19, 1883 and Richmond R. White and William Pierce, Jr. Affidavit in Support of Pension, December 28, 1882, Matteson Pension File.

My husband is of feeble health and unable to support himself and me and we are both so feeble and old that we must suffer if we cannot get help from some source and as our son gave his life for his country, we are now in our old age left without his help and care. We have *no letters* written by him whilst in the service they have all been destroyed, our property is *mortgaged* and our income is not sufficient to support us. Our son before he enlisted gave us his entire wages and he sent us what money he could up to his death.[17]

While she proved that her son died in the war, Rhoda had equally challenging time providing evidence that she was indigent.

Because she did not have any of her son's letters to show that he sent cash home, and she was still married, Rhoda found it very difficult to establish that she needed her mother's pension. Ill with tuberculosis since 1864, Henry Matteson was nearly totally disabled, and unable to farm and complete "hard labor." His taxes continued to increase, and his sister gave him some abutting property to help support the family, but the income from this was only bringing in around $125.00 per year in 1875, hardly enough to support the family. When asked to provide even more evidence of her financial condition, Rhoda wrote in yet another heart wrenching plea for support, "There has been *no* person *legally* bound to support her and that she has been supported by her children and her neighbors. Her husband is sick and has not been able to do any thing during the winter past and that the probability is that he will not be able to do anything for a long time if ever." Rhoda feared about selling off all of her property and being forced to go to the town farm in Scituate for support if she did not receive a pension.[18]

---

[17] Rhoda Matteson, Claimant's Testimony, June 6, 1883, Matteson Pension File.

[18] Edwin L. Leash and Russell A. Watson, Neighbors and General Purpose Affidavit, October 12, 1883, Matteson Pension File. Rhoda Matteson, Claimant's Testimony, March 19, 1883, Matteson Pension File.

Although Henry had sought medical treatment, it did little to relieve his tuberculosis, an almost death sentence in rural Rhode Island at the time. The Pension Bureau wrote yet another letter to Rhoda, asking her for proof from her neighbors that Henry was disabled and unable to provide for her. In a letter dated July 1, 1883, an acting commissioner wrote, "The evidence filed showing the husband's ability to provide for claimant is too indefinite. If no medical evidence is obtainable, then the testimony of neighbors will be considered if the nature and extent of disability is shown, also when, by where, and for what any medical treatment had been rendered between 1863 and 1875." Furthermore, they wanted to know the extent of Henry's property, and the value of his crops.[19]

Additional neighbors came to support Rhoda, as Henry Jackman and Orlando Salisbury wrote, "We know that he is a *very feeble* man as to bodily health being unable to perform any hard manual labor and *unable to support himself and family* and that he and his wife are not possessed of *sufficient property to support themselves comfortably.*" The pension agents seemed concerned that Henry Matteson owned a large amount of land. Amasa Colvin and Harly Phillips, neighbors for over twenty years wrote, "The income from his real estate is small, he being unable to properly improve it on account of his feeble health, and not possessed of sufficient means to have it done, averaging about ten bushels of corn a year, and forty bushels of potatos, besides a small garden."[20]

Rhoda was fortunate to have Dr. Albert Sprague of Warwick come forward to provide an affidavit. Dr. Sprague served in the Civil War as the assistant surgeon of the Seventh Rhode Island and wrote. "I am acquainted with the said Henry

---

[19] Michael Bell, *Food for the Dead: On the Trail of New England's Vampires.* (Middletown, CT: Wesleyan University Press, 2011), 22-25. Acting Commissioner, Pension Bureau to Rhoda Matteson, July 1, 1883, Matteson Pension File.

[20] Henry L. Jackman and Orlando C. Salisbury, Affidavit for Neighbors and General Purposes, August 19, 1883, Matteson Pension File. Amasa Colvin and Harley C. Phillips, Affidavit for Neighbors and General Purposes, June 6, 1883.

Matteson, that I have treated him at various times for the last seven years for pneumonia, incapacitating him from labor for long periods, and that he is now partially disabled." While Rhoda and Henry had several children, one neighbor noted that their children did not support their parents and that the elderly couple had to rely on credit at local stores, as well as the generosity of neighbors. While he owned nearly seventy acres of land, only three acres were farmable. When able to work, Henry's farming only brought in about fifty dollars per year. Many of their bills went unpaid, and they did not have much physical property. None of the affiants wrote about how the death of James affected the family, rather it was the loss of the income he provided his mother, and how his absence affected her ability to live by not providing the family with an income that he had previously earned as a farmer and a soldier.[21]

Rhoda Matteson filed for her pension on August 6, 1879. After a six-year battle to prove that her son died serving his country in the Civil War, and that she was indigent, Rhoda was finally approved for her mother's pension on December 12, 1885. Perhaps as a consolation from the government her son died to save, she received a one-time payment of $2,152 dollars, which represented eight dollars per month from October 1864 through March 1886. For all the years of service, she paid her pension agent George E. Lemore twenty-five dollars for his assistance. Beginning on April 2, 1886, a check for twelve dollars per month was mailed directly to the Hope Post Office, in Scituate. Rhoda continued to receive her pension of twelve dollars per month until June 4, 1893, when she was unceremoniously "Dropped from the Rolls: Pensioner Dead."[22]

---

[21] Albert Sprague, General Affidavit for Any Purpose, March 13, 1882, Matteson Pension File. William P. Hopkins, *The Seventh Regiment Rhode Island Volunteers in the Civil War, 1862-1865*. (Providence: Snow & Farnham, 1903), 334. Bowen Reynolds, General Affidavit, September 28, 1885, Matteson Pension File. William Pierce, Jr, General Affidavit for Any Purpose, September 20, 1882, Matteson Pension File.
[22] Dependent Parents Worksheet, April 2, 1886 and Death Notice, June 4, 1893, both in Matteson Pension File.

Why did it take Rhoda Matteson six years to obtain a pension? In one of the cruel twists of history, there happened to be two men named James Matteson who were shot at Cedar Creek, and they both came from Rhode Island!

Private James A. Matteson was the son of Henry and Rhoda Matteson. A farmer from Scituate, he served in Battery C, First Rhode Island Light Artillery. Private Matteson, as evidenced above was shot in the head at Cedar Creek, and died on October 20, 1864 at the hospital of the Sixth Corps Artillery Brigade. His body was never identified, and likely he rests in an unmarked grave at Winchester National Cemetery.

There was also a Private James Matteson (sometimes spelled Mathewson) who served in Battery G, First Rhode Island Light Artillery. This soldier was born on September 13, 1844 in North Kingstown. He was the son of Verbadus and Mary Ann Greene Matteson. His half-brother, Nicholas Whitford Mattewson (he spelled his name Mathewson, rather than Matteson) and full brother Calvin Rhodes Matteson served in the Seventh Rhode Island. Nicholas was killed in action at Fredericksburg on December 13, 1862. Calvin was wounded there and was discharged. He later reenlisted in the Third Rhode Island Cavalry in 1863, and drowned in December 1864 when the steamer *North America* sank off of Cape Hatteras carrying him home from the war. The James Matteson of Battery G was also a farmer, who enlisted on November 12, 1861; at the time he was living in Coventry, which confuses the situation even more, as it is near Scituate. Private Matteson was wounded at Cedar Creek, and sent to the general hospital, which confused the Pension Bureau clerk into thinking it was James A. Matteson who had been sent there. The James Matteson of Coventry survived his wounds and returned to North Kingstown, where he married Hannah Hazard and died on December 13, 1905; he is buried in Elm Grove Cemetery. [23]

---

[23] Hopkins, *Seventh Rhode Island,* 401-402. Find-A-Grave entry for James Matteson (1844-1905), accessed June 8, 2016. Descriptive Book, Battery G, First Rhode Island Light Artillery, Rhode Island State Archives.

It is not surprising that given the nature of his death, that Private James A. Matteson, like many Rhode Islanders who died in the war, was not listed among his fallen comrades on the 1871 Soldiers and Sailors Monument in Providence. [24] In the late 1880s, Rhode Island began to review the Civil War records, attempting to correct the abysmal reporting system that had been in place during the Civil War. In the 1893 *Revised Register of Rhode Island Volunteers,* the following listing was made for this soldier:

Battery C, First Rhode Island Light Artillery

Mattison, James A., Priv. Res., Scituate, R.I.; Aug. 25, 1861, enrolled; Aug. 25, 1861, mustered in; Dec. 21, 1863, discharged, by reason of reenlistment; Dec. 22, 1863, re-enlisted as Vet. Vol. Granted furlough of thirty-five days from Dec. 25, 1863; Oct. 19, 1864, wounded in the battle of Cedar Creek, Va and sent to the hospital of the Art. Brig, 6th Army Corps. Investigation fails to elicit further information. [25]

Perhaps General William Tecumseh Sherman said it best when he stated, "I think I understand what military fame is; to be killed on the field of battle and have your name misspelled in the newspapers."

In 1913, fifty years after the war, Scituate finally dedicated the Owen Soldier's Monument as a memorial to "the loyal men of Scituate, 1861-1865, who Died in the Service." Scituate had lost many of her sons serving in the First Rhode Island Light Artillery, and it was only appropriate that the monument was an artilleryman, resting with his implement upon a

---

[24] Rhode Island. *Proceedings at the Dedication of the Soldiers and Sailors Monument, in Providence: To Which Is Appended a List of the Deceased Soldiers and Sailors Whose Names Are Sculptured Upon the Monument.* (Providence: A.C. Greene, 1871), 61-62.

[25] Elisha Dyer, *Annual Report of the Adjutant General of Rhode Island and Providence Plantations for the Year 1865. Cor., Rev., and Republished.* (Providence: E.L. Freeman & Son, 1893), 807

shaft, inscribed with the names of the Scituate men who died in the Civil War. Although not listed on the monument in Providence, it was clear from the testimony of his neighbors in Rhoda's pension application that James A. Matteson died in the Civil War and that he had lived his entire life before the war in Scituate. Although he was a soldier from Scituate, his native town neglected him as well, and his name was not recorded on the monument.[26]

Private James A. Matteson rests in an unknown grave in Virginia. His name does not appear on any monument, and except for his pension file, his story would be lost to history. Although he never came home, perhaps the inscription carved on the Owen Soldier's Monument in Scituate to the other men of the town who died "so that nation might live" in the Rebellion is a fitting epitaph for Private James A. Mattison of Battery C, First Rhode Island Light Artillery.

"Rest Soldier, in thine honored grave,
Thy duty nobly done;
Long as thy Country's banners wave,
The land whose life thou diedst to save,
Shall bless the memory of the brave
And prize her patriot sons."[27]

---

[26] Gideon A. Burgess, *Dedication Services: Owen Soldier's Monument.* (Scituate: E.F. Sibley, 1913), 3-4:17-19,
[27] Burgess, *Owen Soldier's Monument,* 7.

Chapter Eight:

In search of Private Coman

On a hot, muggy July afternoon in 2005, I, along with two other members of Colonel Zenas Randall Bliss, Camp 12 of the Department of Rhode Island, Sons of Union Veterans of the Civil War set out into a farmer's field in Glocester hauling a 300-pound block of white marble. We were going to replace the memorial of Private William A. Coman of Company C, Seventh Rhode Island Volunteers who was mortally wounded in the Seventh's valiant, but fruitless charge at Fredericksburg on December 13, 1862. The previous year, one of our members who put a small American flag on the graves of all the Civil War veterans in Glocester had noticed that Coman's stone, which is a cenotaph, was severely deteriorated. As the Veterans Administration will provide a headstone to replace those in this condition, Bliss Camp decided to replace the stone located in the Coman-Bowen Lot, Glocester Cemetery #48 on Elmdale Road in Glocester on property that abuts the popular Barden Family Farm. Aside from hauling the heavy stone through the woods and tangling with thick briars, the installation was easy compared to others we had done- in one incident in Burrillville, we were unsure if were in Rhode Island, Connecticut, or Massachusetts.

When I returned home that night to Warwick, I pulled my well-worn copy of William Palmer Hopkins' *The Seventh Regiment Rhode Island Volunteers in the Civil War: 1862-1865* to discover what information I could on Coman. Hopkins had spent nearly forty years compiling biographical material on members of the regiment. As William Coman had served in the same Company C as my third great uncle, Alfred Sheldon Knight of Scituate, I was particularly interested. Hopkins wrote the following brief biography of Coman:

William Arnold Coman, son of William and Pulcharia Savalla Steere Coman, was born Jan. 4, 1836, in Glocester, R.I. He was the sixth of eight children, all of whom are now dead. William was a farmer by occupation and resided in his native town most of the time previous to his enlistment. Oct. 17, 1856, he married Frances Adelaide Douglas, a native of Thompson, Windham County, Conn. They had four children: Arthur Clinton, who died in babyhood, George Everett, Estella Maria, who died in her twenty-eighth year, and William Elmer. The two survivors are druggists. William Arnold was a wagoner until a few days before the battle of Fredericksburg. Just prior to that engagement he wrote his wife the roads were so bad he was tired of the team, that he would not be in more danger in the ranks, and that he should try to get returned to his company. That was the last she heard from him. After the battle his captain wrote her that he was missing. She never ascertained the particulars of his death. He was mortally wounded and evidently survived but a short time. His widow desires to learn if anyone saw him after he was wounded.[1]

In the summer of 2007, I began my first of three fantastic summers working as a National Park Ranger in Virginia. Assigned to Harpers Ferry National Park, each day was spent giving tours and doing research related to the Civil War. On my days off however, I would drive throughout Virginia to visit the many battlefields there. My first day off took me to Fredericksburg for the first time, where the Seventh Rhode Island had its bloody baptism by fire, losing forty percent of the regiment, including forty-nine dead or mortally wounded. No Rhode Island regiment in any battle of any war ever sustained the number of casualties that the Seventh did at Fredericksburg. In my first visit, I found the locations where the Seventh fought, now all paved over, including a gas station where the regiment hunkered down to escape the murderous fire of Marye's Heights.

---

[1] William P. Hopkins, *The Seventh Regiment Rhode Island Volunteers in the Civil War: 1862-1865.* (Providence: Snow & Farnum, 1903), 382.

After visiting what was left of the battlefield, I walked to the top of Marye's Heights to the Fredericksburg National Cemetery, searching for Rhode Island soldiers. I quickly discovered the graves of several Seventh Rhode Island men who had died at Spotsylvania Court House. As I walked the long rows of small granite blocks, I did not doubt that there were dozens of Rhode Islanders buried here who will be forever labeled as "Unknown." Scanning the ground at my feet, I made an amazing discovery. There was a small granite marker that simply read "4899 W.A. Coman RI." It was the grave of Private William A. Coman of Company C, Seventh Rhode Island Volunteers.[2]

Not much is known about the early life of William A. Coman. He is not listed in the census of 1840, 1850, or 1860. Coman was a farmer before the war in Glocester. The Coman family was among the earliest settlers of the town and is sometimes referred to as the "Comer" family in early records.[3]

On October 17, 1856, Coman, then twenty-one married Frances Douglass of nearby Scituate in a religious ceremony performed by the Rev. George T. Day in Johnston. He took his bride back to Glocester and fathered five children. We know that in 1862, he was living in the southeastern corner of Glocester, on what later became Elmdale Road, near the Scituate line. Among his crops were numerous apple trees, which are still harvested by Rhode Islanders today. In a later history of the town, one writer referred to Glocester farmers as being "industrious and frugal."[4]

William A. Coman entered the history pages on August 4, 1862 to enlist as a member of what later became Company C of

---

[2] Interment records, Fredericksburg National Cemetery, Fredericksburg and Spotsylvania National Military Park, Fredericksburg, VA.
[3] Elizabeth A. Perry, *A Brief History of Glocester, Rhode Island.* Edited by Edna Whitaker Kent. (Bowie, MD: Heritage Books, 1995), 75-76.
[4] 1840, 1850, and 1860 United States Census, Glocester, Rhode Island. Marriage Certificate of William A. and Frances Coman, William A. Coman Pension File, National Archives. Site visit to the Coman-Bowen Lot, Glocester Cemetery #48, Glocester, RI. Perry, *History of Glocester,* 51.

the Seventh Rhode Island Volunteers. Although recruitment efforts for the Seventh had begun in earnest in May 1862, it was not until President Lincoln issued a serious call for volunteers in July 1862 that the recruitment effort picked up. In order to spur enlistments, Glocester offered a bounty of four hundred dollars to raise recruits for the Seventh. Whether it was patriotism or the want to secure a nest egg for his family, Coman went to Chepachet and enlisted to serve three years. An examining surgeon recorded that Coman was five feet ten and one-half inches tall, had a dark complexion, with hazel eyes and brown hair. Company C was ably led by Captain George E. Church who was an engineer by training and had seen combat, fighting native peoples in Argentina. The bulk of the company was recruited in Glocester and also included men who had joined in Providence and later been assigned to the company. The overwhelming majority of the men in Company C were farmers and their age varied from 18 to 49, with the vast majority being in their mid-twenties. After a few weeks of training at Camp Bliss in Providence, the Seventh left Rhode Island for Virginia.[5]

Assigned to the First Brigade, Second Division, Ninth Corps, the Seventh spent several weeks in Washington and in nearby Maryland training and preparing for active field service. No known wartime letters from Coman survive, but his experiences would have been similar to the rest of the men in the regiment, as they learned to drill, adapted to the course food of the army, and realized that war was not a holiday sport as a typhoid epidemic killed several men from Hopkinton early in the service. Finally, by late October 1862, the Army of the Potomac was on the move again, as the Seventh Rhode Island marched south to a city called Fredericksburg, which blocked their path to Richmond.

---

[5] Enlistment Paper of William A. Coman, Rhode Island State Archives. Muster in rolls and descriptive book, Company C, Seventh Rhode Island Volunteers, Rhode Island State Archives. Hopkins, *Seventh Rhode Island,* 315-319. For an excellent set of letters from a man in Company C from Glocester, refer to the letters of Emor Young transcribed in Kris VanDenBossche, ed. *Write Soon and Give me all the news.* (Peace Dale, RI: Rhode Island Historical Document Transcription Project, 1993), 57-86.

The army, now under the command of adopted Rhode Islander Major General Ambrose Burnside prepared to attack the fortified city as soon as the necessary logistics were in place.[6]

While Private Coman had been excused from duty due to his detail as the company's wagon master, he felt that this was a more hazardous duty than serving in the ranks. Sometime before the battle of Fredericksburg, he asked Captain Church for permission to rejoin the regiment and serve as a rifleman in the ranks; it would be a fatal mistake. On December 13, 1862, the Seventh, along with the rest of the Army of the Potomac attacked the fortified Confederate defenses in the rear of the city. The Seventh Rhode Island went in at 12:20 that afternoon, and instantly came under a murderous bombardment and Confederate musket fire; Rhode Islanders began to be killed, wounded, and maimed as soon as the regiment left the city to begin the assault, still, despite the odds against them, the Seventh stayed together and pushed forward.[7]

Private Alfred Sheldon Knight of Scituate, who served in Company C with Coman, wrote afterwards. "I was on the field about 7 hours Balls and Shells fell in torants but it fell to my lot not yet hurt. There was greate many that went to there long home that day. Our Regt got badly cut up." Taking 570 officers and men into the fighting, the regiment lost forty-nine dead or mortally wounded, 145 wounded in some form, and three men captured, for a total of 197 officers and men; forty percent of those who fought were casualties. Seven of the dead and ten of the wounded were from Company C. Captain Lewis Leavens of Hopkinton best summed up the loss when he wrote, "Scarce a man but lost a friend or relative."[8]

_____

[6] Alfred Sheldon Knight to William Warren Knight, September 14, 1862 and to Horace Ralph, September 21, 1862, author's collection. Hopkins, *Seventh Rhode Island,* 33-40.
[7] Hopkins, *Seventh Rhode Island,* 41-49.
[8]Thomas F. Tobey to John Tobey, December 20, 1862, Tobey Papers, Beinecke Library, Yale University, New Haven, CT. Alfred Sheldon Knight to Horace Ralph, December 21, 1862 and William Warren

As the men regrouped in their winter camp at Falmouth, Virginia after the battle, they realized that the battle had been a useless waste of life. Drummer William Palmer Hopkins of West Greenwich recalled, "The slaughter was over. The army was decimated and despondent. The soldiers felt more accurately than words can indicate that their assaults had been fruitless and that their comrades had died in vain." Soldiers gathered in their log huts and around campfires comparing stories, inquiring who had been killed or wounded, trying to determine what had become of their comrades who were simply listed "missing in action." Because of the gruesome nature of Civil War combat, and the murderous artillery bombardment that the Seventh had endured, the majority of those dead had been maimed to such an extent that they could not be identified. Because the army had hastily retreated back across the Rappahannock River after the battle, none of the dead from the Seventh, with the exception of Lieutenant Colonel Welcome B. Sayles were recovered. When several members of regiment re-crossed the river under a flag of truce, they discovered that the dead had been stripped of all identifying documents, making identification impossible. Nearly all the members of the Seventh Rhode Island who were killed in action at Fredericksburg were buried as unknowns, while for some; a cenotaph was erected in their memory in a cemetery in Rhode Island.[9]

For the wounded, a terrible fate awaited them, as they were transported back across the river and sent first to the regimental hospital and later to hospitals around Washington. The Seventh was blessed to have three of the most competent doctors in Rhode Island serving in the ranks, however, even these talented physicians could not keep up with the terrible toll of battle, as men continued to die of the wounds they suffered in the battle; the

---

Knight, December 28, 1862, author's collection." *Narragansett Weekly,* December 25, 1862.
[9] Hopkins, *Seventh Rhode Island,* 50-51. Zenas R. Bliss, *The Reminiscences of Major General Zenas R. Bliss: 1854-1876.* Edited by Thomas T. Smith, Jerry D. Thompson, Robert Wooster, and Ben E. Pingenot. (Austin: Texas State Historical Association, 2007), 327-334.

horrible injuries were beyond the medical capabilities of the time. For those lucky enough to make it to a hospital alive, and who later died of their injuries, their deaths were recorded, and the men received a proper burial with a marked grave, or their remains were shipped back to Rhode Island.[10]

Dr. James Harris was the surgeon of the Seventh, holding the rank of major. Attending Brown University briefly before the war, he had graduated from the University of New York and later attended medical school at the Philadelphia College of Medicine and Surgery, graduating in 1852. He had performed a residency in New York City, and went to the Crimea in 1855, serving as a contract surgeon with the Russian forces, learning battlefield surgery firsthand. He served in the First Rhode Island Detached Militia in 1861, and was captured at Bull Run, rather than abandon his patients. After his release, Harris organized the Portsmouth Grove Hospital, and in the summer of 1862, was appointed surgeon of the Seventh. Having long served as a military doctor, Major Harris knew that adequate records were a key part of his work, as his patients or their families could use his records to later obtain a pension.[11]

With the permission of Colonel Zenas R. Bliss, Harris demanded that every company commander in the Seventh send in a full return of those men from their company who had been killed or wounded at Fredericksburg. Every company commander complied with the order, providing detailed descriptions of the fate of the soldiers under their command, detailing their wounds, and to which hospital the wounded were sent. Immediately after the battle Captain Church had been promoted to lieutenant colonel of the regiment, leaving Lieutenant James Potter in charge of Company C. Potter deferred the task of completing the report of First Sergeant Henry Lincoln who simply tore out a blank sheet of

---

[10] Returns of Company A, Seventh Rhode Island Volunteers, December 1862 and January 1863, author's collection. Stephen F. Peckham, "Recollections of a Hospital Steward in the Civil War," Newport Historical Society, Newport, RI. Hopkins, *Seventh Rhode Island,* 48-51.
[11] Hopkins, *Seventh Rhode Island,* 332-333. James Harris Papers, Rhode Island Historical Society.

paper and labeled it "List of killed, wounded, and missing in Co. C." Although none of his comrades had seen him on the battlefield, Sergeant Lincoln recorded on the list "Wm A. Coman. Mortally." Coman was carried on the muster rolls of the Seventh as "Missing in Action at the Battle of Fredericksburg Va," until March 1863, when his status was changed to "Killed Dec. 13th, 1862."[12]

News was slow to arrive back home in Glocester. The town was and remains a rural outpost in the smallest state. Only a single telegraph wire ran to Chepachet, and the mail was always especially slow in bringing news from the front. The local *Providence Journal* published the names of those killed and wounded at Fredericksburg, but did not record any information about Private Coman. At some point in January 1863, the sad news finally arrived at the Coman farm on Elmdale Road that Frances Coman was now a widow, and her children were orphans.[13]

With the passage of new pension legislation on July 14, 1862, Frances Coman was eligible to collect William's back pay, bounty, as well as a pension to support her and her children. She began the process by contacting the office of Joseph Story Pitman in Providence. Pitman, a Providence attorney who had served in the First Rhode Island Detached Militia assisted Rhode Island families through the complicated process of obtaining a government pension. In her initial filing, dated July 7, 1863 Frances went to the Federal court house in Providence and submitted a copy of the company muster roll and her marriage certificate to the pension office; her filing was given number 7369 in the "War of 1861," while listing her post office address as Harmony, Rhode Island. She gave the names of the children, and

---

[12] Returns of casualties, Battle of Fredericksburg, Seventh Rhode Island Volunteers, in Harris papers. Bi-monthly muster rolls for Company C, Seventh Rhode Island Volunteers, January-February and March-April 1863, National Archives.

[13] *Providence Journal,* December 19-30, 1862. Edna M. Kent, *Glocester: The Way Up Country.* (Glocester: Glocester Bicentennial Commission, 1976), 54. Coman pension file.

swore before a clerk she had not remarried since learning of William's death. The clerk gathered the documents and sent them to the Department of the Interior's Pension Bureau to await adjudication.[14]

While Glocester was quick to pay out the bounty owed to William, Frances' application began to be worked by the overburdened clerks in Washington. A clerk wrote to the Adjutant General's Office in Washington, asking for additional evidence of the service and death of William Coman. On August 16, 1863 the reply came in the form of a letter from the Adjutant General's Office who wrote that "He is reported as Missing in Action since battle of Fredericksburg, VA. His name is not borne on any subsequent rolls of that Company on file. No evidence of death on file."[15]

Without evidence of his death, the Pension Bureau needed additional evidence that Private Coman was dead. Frances reached out to now Captain James N. Potter, who had commanded Company C after the battle. Because of the volunteer nature of Civil War regiments, one of the duties of the officers was to provide affidavits of support to help their men and their families obtain the government benefits they were entitled to. Oftentimes officers devoted much of their spare time to writing these documents. On August 25, 1863, Captain Potter was in Providence and wrote the following affidavit:

> I certify on honor that I was a commissioned officer in said Company that at that time at Fredericksburgh, Va the said William A. Coman while in the service of the United States and in the line of duty was wounded severely in the battle at that place, as he was reported to me by members of the company. I saw him in the company when we marched on the field + that is the last I ever saw of him. He is reported as missing in action to the best of my

[14] Declaration for Widow's Pension, Frances Coman, in Coman pension file.
[15] Adjutant General's Office to Pension Office, August 14, 1863, Coman pension file.

knowledge + belief said Coman died on the field that day from his wounds. Such to was reported to me he had received. I had made diligent enquiry respecting him + this is the conclusion to which my mind was brought.[16]

Captain Potter's affidavit proved the tipping point in the case, and October 27, 1863, Frances Coman began receiving checks at the Harmony Post Office in the amount of eight dollars per month to support her, with the claim backdated to December 13, 1862.[17]

While Frances received eight dollars per month, her children received nothing in the initial filing. On September 10, 1866, Frances again returned to the court and filed a "Widow's Application for an Increase of Pension." She again presented her marriage certificate from the town clerk in Johnston and listed the names of her children and their birthdates. Frances had been pregnant when William enlisted and gave birth to her final child on December 18, 1862, naming him William Elmer Coman. She presented two neighbors as witnesses, Charles O. Barnes and Elizabeth F. Chamberlain of Glocester. Elizabeth was familiar with this process, as her husband, First Sergeant Bradford Chamberlain of Company I, Second Rhode Island Volunteers had died fighting at Spotsylvania Court House in May 1864.[18]

The pension adjudicators took Frances' latest affidavit and approved an increase in the pension effective March 19, 1867. Now she received an additional two dollars per month, per child, until they turned sixteen. Frances would remain eligible for her

---

[16] James N. Potter, affidavit in support of Frances Coman, August 25, 1863, Coman pension file. For more information on officer correspondence to families see the letters to families in the James Harris and James Remington at the Rhode Island Historical Society.

[17] Frances Coman Declaration for Pension, Coman pension file.

[18] Frances Coman, Widow's Application for Pension Increase and marriage certificate, Coman pension file. Town of Glocester, Rhode Island, birth, marriage, and death records, 1861-1866, Glocester Town Hall, Glocester, RI. Augustus Woodbury, *The Second Rhode Island Regiment: A Narrative of Military Operations.* (Providence: Valpey, Angell, and Company, 1875), 410

pension as long as she did not remarry. At some point, she erected a simple marble cenotaph in the family cemetery in the apple orchard, still not knowing exactly what happened to her husband. In 1865, a Rhode Island state census worker found her residing in Glocester with Corliss and Eliza Coman, along with her children, George, Estella, and William. The census taker tersely noted she was the "Widow of Wm. Killed in War."[19]

Frances continued to scrape by, being supported by her children, trying to live on her meager eight dollar a month pension. She did not receive an increase until new pension legislation was enacted in September 1916, when she petitioned the government for an increase; she was still residing in Glocester at this time. The increase was approved and she began collecting twenty dollars per month beginning October 27, 1916, which was finally increased to thirty dollars per month. Throughout her decades of widowhood, Frances remained attached to her family. While family members of other Seventh Rhode Island soldiers regularly attended the reunions of the Seventh Rhode Island Veterans Association, no member of the Coman family ever did. Several Seventh veterans lived nearby to the Coman family, but they never provided the needed information sought. On May 18, 1923, the postmaster at the North Scituate post office, where Frances' pension checks had been sent for so long returned her latest check to the Pension Bureau, stating she had died on April 9, 1923. Frances Coman was laid to rest in a quiet corner of the family cemetery, next to the cenotaph she had erected so many years previous. She never knew what happened to her beloved husband who died serving in the Seventh Rhode Island down in Virginia.[20]

---

[19] Frances Coman "Claim for Increase of Widow's Pension," March 19, 1867, "Coman pension file. 1865 Rhode Island Census, Town of Glocester, Rhode Island State Archives.

[20] "Drop Report-Pensioner," June 4, 1923, and Frances Coman, application for pension increase, September 1916, all in Coman pension file. Register and Minutes of the Seventh Rhode Island Veterans Association, 1873-1923, author's collection.

So how did Private William A. Coman end up buried in grave 4899 at Fredericksburg National Cemetery? As the Seventh Rhode Island advanced steadily into an unrelenting barrage of artillery and musket fire at Fredericksburg, Coman was shot in the left lung and dropped to the ground. No soldier in the Seventh Rhode Island could stop to help their disabled comrade. After the Seventh fell back from its position in front of the sunken road on Marye's Heights on the night of December 13, 1862, they retreated back to the city of Fredericksburg. While the Seventh was pinned down in front of Marye's Heights, General Burnside kept up the assault against Marye's Heights. At 3:30 that afternoon, the First Division of the Fifth Corps went into action to support the Ninth Corps. After the Fifth Corps was repulsed, it was nearly sundown. With the firing calming down finally, on this part of the field, stretcher bearers and ambulances were able to go onto the field and retrieve the wounded. The Twenty-Second Massachusetts of the Fifth Corps had charged over the same ground as the Seventh Rhode Island. A member of the regiment recalled the horrifying condition as the sunset on December 13, 1862:

> The ground was freezing; and the wounded, to be rescued, must be reached before they chilled to death. Many of the dead of Rhode Island were about us, and we literally slept on them. They were groaning, imploring, and screaming, several in their last death-agonies. Their distressed, harsh, rattling breathing told us of the near approach of the Grim Destroyer.[21]

 With limited room in the wagons, only the wounded could be brought back across the river to await a surgeon's care, the dead were left where they fell. During the course of the search for the wounded, Coman was retrieved by men from the First Division,

---

[21] John L. Parker and Robert G. Carter, *Henry Wilson's Regiment: History of the Twenty-Second Massachusetts Infantry, The Second Company Sharpshooters, and the Third Light Battery, in the War of the Rebellion.* (Boston: Press of the Rand Avery Company, 1887), 229.

Fifth Corps. Late that night he was taken back across the Rappahannock River. [22]

Coman was admitted to the general hospital of the First Division, Fifth Corps in the early morning hours of December 14, 1862. Here he was seen by an unknown surgeon. Shot in the left lung, all a doctor could do was to make him comfortable; it was a mortal wound. Someone who treated Coman noted that he was a private in the Seventh Rhode Island. In extreme agony, he died of his wounds on December 19, 1862 and was laid to rest on the Philip's Farm near Falmouth, Virginia. His grave was adequately marked so that in 1866 he was buried in a marked grave at Fredericksburg National Cemetery. It is a fitting location for so many members of the Seventh Rhode Island to be buried, on top of the hill they tried so desperately to seize that December day in 1862.[23]

It was a breakdown in the lines of communications that allowed Frances Coman to suffer all her life inquiring about her husband. Because William Coman had been treated in a hospital of a different unit, his death was not immediately reported to the officers of the Seventh Rhode Island. In the aftermath of the battle, his comrades could only speculate about his fate, as they had seen him fall to the ground, with what they assumed to be a mortal wound. No Fifth Corps officer ever reported to any member of the Seventh that he had died on December 19; as such William was listed as missing in action, until he was declared dead in which to enable Frances to collect her pension. While several Seventh Rhode Island veterans are known to have visited Fredericksburg National Cemetery after the war, they never noticed the marked grave of Private Coman. Although the letters are lost to history, his death was recorded in the 1893 *Revised Register of Rhode Island Volunteers* as "mortally wounded at Fredericksburg, Va.,

---

[22] Interment record of Private William A. Coman, Grave 4899, Fredericksburg National Cemetery, Fredericksburg, VA. Francis A. O' Reilly, *The Fredericksburg Campaign: Winter War on the Rappahannock.* (Baton Rouge: Louisiana State University Press, 2003), 364-368.
[23] Coman Interment record.

and died Dec. 19, 1862." While the massive volume lists Rhode Island soldiers buried in several National Cemeteries in the South, no mention is made of those interred at Fredericksburg National Cemetery. Captain James N. Potter died of illness he contracted in the service in 1869 and provided no additional information to the Coman family.[24]

Throughout much of the late nineteenth century, Drummer William Hopkins devoted much of his spare time to studying the history of his former regiment, retraveling the path of his regiment, and gathering letters and photographs to write a history with. Hopkins was meticulous in his research and wrote countless letters to comrades and the families of Seventh Rhode Island veterans seeking information to write biographical sketches of many members of the regiment. Hopkins was in touch with the Coman family and wrote the brief sketch presented at the beginning of the article. It was clear that as late as 1903, when his book *The Seventh Regiment Rhode Island Volunteers in the Civil War* was published, no member of the regiment could recall what had happened to Private Coman, and Frances continued to seek out information. In his register of Company C, Hopkins copied verbatim from the 1893 *Revised Register*. As time passed, and more Seventh Rhode Island veterans went with it, Private Coman was all but forgotten, resting in a marked grave in Virginia.[25]

By being taken to a hospital of a different unit, the fate of Private William A. Coman was nearly lost to the pages of history. Fortunately, he was able to make it to a field hospital before dying, thus enabling his identity to be recorded and be buried in a marked grave at Fredericksburg National Cemetery. In 1871, the State of Rhode Island placed William's name on the Soldiers and Sailors Monument in Providence, thus recognizing him as an official Civil War fatality from Rhode Island. A decade after it was placed, the new cenotaph continues to be present in the Coman family

---

[24] Elisha Dyer Jr., *Revised Register of Rhode Island Volunteers: Volume I.* (Providence: E.L. Freeman, 1893), 356: 710-713. Hopkins, *Seventh Rhode Island,* 352.
[25] Hopkins, *Seventh Rhode Island,* xi-xiii: 382: 455. William P. Hopkins papers, author's collection.

cemetery, a simple block of white marble that serves as a memorial to a farmer who went to war to save the Union and never came back. Besides this stone is the grave of Frances A. Coman who waited for the rest of her life for news about her husband. Hopefully, she can finally rest in peace.

Chapter Nine:

Writing Rhode Island Civil War History

With the firing on Fort Sumter on April 12, 1861 Rhode Islanders eagerly answered the call to arms. From Westerly to Woonsocket, Wallum Lake to Little Compton, the men from Rhode Island went to war. When it was over the smallest state in the Union had sent to the war eight regiments of infantry, three heavy artillery regiments, three regiments and a squadron of cavalry, ten batteries of light artillery, as well as hundreds of men who served in the United States Navy, Army, and Marine Corps. Rhode Islanders served in nearly every major battle of the war, firing the first infantry shots at Bull Run, and some of the last by the cavalry at Appomattox. Roughly 23,000 Rhode Islanders enlisted in the Civil War, over 2,000 gave the ultimate sacrifice.[1]

From 1862 until the second decade of the twentieth century, the soldiers and sailors of Rhode Island also left an indelible mark on the pages of history by writing and publishing many histories of their participation in the Civil War. Indeed, with the exception of Batteries C and G, First Rhode Island Light Artillery and the Second and Third Rhode Island Cavalry Regiments, every unit sent from Rhode Island published a history written by men who served in the unit. Over the last century these veteran published sources were added to by scores of other books and articles by scholars, buffs, and those interested in Rhode Island's role in the Civil War. Indeed, Rhode Island has perhaps the greatest written record of any northern state in the Civil War era.

---

[1] For a good overview of the Rhode Island Civil War experience, refer to Robert Grandchamp, *Rhode Island and the Civil War: Voices from the Ocean State.* (Charleston: History Press, 2012)

In 1862, Augustus Woodbury published *A Narrative of the Campaign of the First Rhode Island Regiment in the Spring and Summer of 1861*. This book was the *first* published regimental history written by a participant in the Civil War. Woodbury, who served in the First Rhode Island Detached Militia as the regimental chaplain set the gold standard by which all future regimental histories were and are written. He placed the role of the First Rhode Island within the context of the Bull Run Campaign and focused heavily on the participation of the regiment in the engagement. Woodbury included a complete roster of the First Rhode Island and included short biographies of the officers and men who perished in the service. As the war was still being fought, Woodbury also listed men from the regiment who had reenlisted in other units.[2]

In 1864, Edwin W. Stone, who served in Battery C, First Rhode Island Light Artillery, published *Rhode Island in the Rebellion*. During the war, Stone served as a correspondent to the *Providence Journal,* writing detailed letters about his experiences in the Army of the Potomac. The book was published in early 1864, and only contains Stone's letters written through Gettysburg. Despite this, *Rhode Island in the Rebellion* is a valuable resource. Nearly a third of book is an appendix in which are brief histories of each Rhode Island regiment and battery. Stone did not write these histories himself, rather a member of each unit wrote the history for inclusion in the book. These histories present a remarkable view of the war, as it was going on by the participants. In addition, Stone also included brief biographies of several Rhode Island soldiers who died in the war. *Rhode Island in the Rebellion* was reissued in 1865 with the inclusion of a chapter on the events of 1864 and additional biographical material for officers who died in the 1864 campaigns. Often overlooked today, *Rhode Island in the Rebellion* remains a valuable resource.[3]

---

[2] *Newport Mercury,* June 21, 1862.
[3] Edwin M. Stone, *Rhode Island in the Rebellion*. (Providence: George H. Whitney, 1864 and 1865)

Chaplain Woodbury returned to publishing in 1875 by writing the official regimental history of the Second Rhode Island Volunteers. For his work, Woodbury spoke with fellow veterans of the regiment, and was freely given access to both private and personal papers of the soldiers of the Second. The *Providence Journal* recorded, "The historian understood that nothing but the truth and impartiality was sought, and from such a man nothing else could have been obtained, even desired. The narrative is sprightly and told in Mr. Woodbury's happiest style." Chaplain Frederic Denison who served in both the First Rhode Island Cavalry and the Third Rhode Island Heavy Artillery published *Sabres and Spurs* and *Shot and Shell* in 1876 and 1879 respectively. Denison, a Brown educated Baptist minister of the "church militant" was also a historian who wrote two excellent histories which are widely considered to still be two of the best sources on the cavalry in the Army of the Potomac, and service in South Carolina. A poet as well, Denison published his poetry in these volumes.[4]

One of the most important sources published by Rhode Islanders was the one hundred papers published in the ten volumes of the *Personal Narratives of Events in the War of the Rebellion: Being papers read before the Rhode Island Soldiers and Sailors Historical Society*. Formed in Providence in 1874, the Soldiers and Sailors Historical Society was composed of veterans who met each month where one of their number would present a historical paper on their military service. One hundred of these papers were issued in paperback form from 1878 until 1915, shortly after which the society disbanded. The *New England Historical and Genealogical Register* recorded, "The society deserves much credit for its labors in preserving the record of events in so important a portion of our national history."

---

[4] *Providence Journal,* March 17, 1875. Frederic Denison, *Sabres and Spurs: The First Regiment Rhode Island Cavalry in the Civil War, 1861-1865. Its Origins, Marches, Scouts, Skirmishes, Raid, Battles, Sufferings, Victories, and Appropriate Official Papers; with The Roll of Honor and Roll of the Regiment.* (Central Falls: E.L. Freeman, 1876)

The papers were collected and published in hardcover in volumes of ten papers, comprising ten full volumes. Publishing the single volumes received praise. "They contain much interesting matter concerning events in the late war for the preservation of the union, which but for this mode of publication would have been lost." It is important to note that not all papers read before the Society were published as many still exist in manuscript form at the Rhode Island Historical Society and Providence Public Library, while others were independently published elsewhere by their authors.

The full set of ten volumes was republished in the 1990s by Broadfoot Publishing as part of their series of war papers from the Military Order of the Loyal Legion of the United States (MOLLUS). Despite this, these papers were not published originally by MOLLUS and Rhode Island never had a MOLLUS Commandery. In addition to this, not all of the papers were written by men who served in Rhode Island units. Because these papers were initially issued individually, they will be listed under the regiments in which their author served.[5]

Prior to 1892, Rhode Islanders had sporadically published sources about their participation in the war. The histories published before were published by and paid for entirely by the veterans or the regimental association. Often published in limited numbers, these books were found in the many mill village libraries throughout the state. In 1890, the veterans of the Fifth Rhode Island Heavy Artillery sent a resolution to the Rhode Island General Assembly asking for a sum of money to help in writing and publishing a regimental history. Beginning in 1892, the Rhode Island General Assembly offered each Rhode Island regimental veteran association six hundred dollars to publish a regimental history of their unit. The state would purchase two hundred copies of the history "for the use of the state," often sending them to

[5] Finding Aid, Rhode Island Soldiers and Sailors Historical Society Papers, MSS 723, Rhode Island Historical Society. "Book Notices." *The New England Historical and Genealogical Register* Vol. 36 (1882), 100-101. "Book Notices." *The New England Historical and Genealogical Register* Vol. 35 (1881), 406.

libraries both in Rhode Island and elsewhere, as well as to veteran's homes and Grand Army of the Republic Posts around the country. In addition, members of the General Assembly and judges of the Rhode Island court system were also given copies to give to their constituents. The generous gift of the Rhode Island General Assembly was the catalyst for the remaining Rhode Island veteran associations to publish regimental histories.[6]

Typical of these histories is the massive 1903 regimental history of the Seventh Rhode Island Volunteers. Raised in 1862, the Seventh saw hard service in both the Army of the Potomac and in Mississippi during the Vicksburg Campaign. The soldiers of the Seventh formed a veteran association in 1873, but did not begin to seriously consider writing a regimental history until 1889 when a committee of twenty-five veterans gathered to write the history. "A committee of so many members was found to be unwieldy and inefficient and accomplished little of importance," wrote one member of the regiment. By 1893, the twenty-five-member committee had accomplished little work in writing the history. Instead, Seventh Rhode Island Veteran Association president, Nathan B. Lewis who had served in the regiment as a corporal and was now a prominent lawyer and judge in Washington County appointed another committee of five members to gather funds to publish the history to supplement the money provided by the state. William P. Hopkins, a former drummer in the regiment was appointed to write the actual history.

Hopkins, now living in Lawrence, Massachusetts was "indefatigable in collecting material for such a work." He wrote thousands of letters to fellow veterans, including Confederates that the Seventh fought against, gathered letters and diaries of fellow veterans from the Seventh, collected hundreds of photographs of regimental comrades, and wrote biographical sketches of most of

---

[6] John K. Burlingame, *History of the Fifth Regiment of Rhode Island Heavy Artillery During Three Years and a Half of Service in North Carolina. January 1862-June 1865.* (Providence: Snow & Farnum, 1892), v-viii. *Acts and Resolves Passed by the General Assembly of the State of Rhode Island and Providence Plantations at the January Session, 1899.* (Providence: E.L. Freeman, 1899), 221-222.

the soldiers in the regiment. Furthermore, Hopkins traveled throughout the South, revisiting the battlefields the Seventh had fought and camped on in Maryland, Virginia, and Mississippi. By the time he was done his research, which took up most of the 1890s, Hopkins "had sufficient material to make a credible history of the regiment."

Hopkins wrote his history of the Seventh Rhode Island and had it edited by Dr. George B. Peck of Providence, himself a veteran of the Second Rhode Island and author of several accounts of his own service. Hopkins wrote, "The result sought in the publication of this volume is to place on record an authentic account of the part performed by the Seventh Rhode Island Regiment in the suppression of the Rebellion and to perpetuate the memory of the heroic men who gave up their lives in the service of their country." When it was published in 1903, *The Seventh Regiment Rhode Island Volunteers in the Civil War, 1862-1865* was widely hailed, and still is, as one of the finest regimental histories published in the post-war period. Filled with hundreds of photographs, biographical sketches, and a main text that reads like a diary from a front-line participant, it is the greatest book ever published on Rhode Island in the Civil War era.[7]

The First Rhode Island Light Artillery regiment was unique in its service. Recruited at the Benefit Street Arsenal in Providence, the eight batteries of the regiment were mustered in one battery at a time and never served together as a full regiment. One veteran jokingly referred to the First Rhode Island Light Artillery as a "geography class" because of its varied service. In July 1863, Batteries A, B, C, E, and G were serving in the Army of the Potomac at Gettysburg. Battery D was stationed in Kentucky with the Ninth Corps, while Battery F was detailed to New Bern, North Carolina, and Battery H served in the defenses of Washington, D.C. Because of the wide and varied service of

---

[7] Seventh Rhode Island Volunteers, Regimental Association Minute Books, 1885-1903, Robert Grandchamp Collection. William P. Hopkins, *The Seventh Regiment Rhode Island Volunteers in the Civil War, 1862-1865*. (Providence: Snow & Farnum, 1903), i-xvi.

these batteries, each unit was authorized to publish a history; all did with the exception of Battery C and Battery G.[8]

Taken together, these regimental histories form one of the most important resources to study Rhode Island in the Civil War period. Written by the men who participated in the unit, they present a detailed, first-hand account of their service. Furthermore, many of the volumes contain engravings or photographs of the officers and men who served in the unit. Of particular importance are biographical sketches and accounts of the actions in which they participated. Sometimes though, these sources must be remembered that they were written in the Victorian era, as they often do not discuss desertions, the high bounties that some men enlisted for, or drunk or incompetent officers. While some of these regimental histories do have their shortcomings in not discussing the dark side of the war, for the most part they provide an honest, day to day view of Rhode Island's Civil War units. The books were widely distributed and varied in cost upon publication, the history of Battery B sold for three dollars, while the history of the Seventh Rhode Island Volunteers originally sold for five dollars. The men who wrote these books often spent more on their publication than what they made in sales. It was a labor of love that led them to recall their unit's part in the Civil War.[9]

After 1917, with the disbandment of the Rhode Island Soldiers and Sailors Historical Society and the passing of many of the state's Civil War veterans, the steady stream of publications about Rhode Island and the Civil War began to decline. In 1964, Brigadier General Harold R. Barker, a veteran of both World Wars whose grandfather had served in the First Rhode Island Detached Militia wrote, *History of Rhode Island Combat Units in the Civil*

---

[8] George B. Peck, *Historical Address Delivered at the Dedication of the Memorial Tablet on the Arsenal Benefit Street, Corner of Meeting Providence, R.I. Thursday July 19, 1917.* (Providence: Rhode Island Print Co., 1917), 5-15.

[9] Advertisement for Battery B, First Rhode Island Light Artillery Regimental History, Gettysburg National Military Park, Gettysburg, PA. *Publisher's Weekly,* April 4, 1903. *Providence Evening Press,* July 21, 1871.

War which served as the official state history to commemorate the centennial of the Civil War. General Barker's book is a compression of the regimental histories published by the veterans after the war. He performed no original research, rather publishing excerpts from the histories to detail the role of a Rhode Island unit in a particular battle. The book is heavily illustrated and also includes details such as Medal of Honor recipients, and the battle honors earned by each regiment. Widely distributed by the state, General Barker's book is still frequently read and is often the first book many read on Rhode Island and the Civil War.[10]

It was not until the 1980s that another round of books on Rhode Island and the Civil War were published. In 1985, Robert Hunt Rhodes, the great-grandson of Colonel Elisha Hunt Rhodes of the Second Rhode Island Volunteers published his ancestor's diary through Mowbray Publishing in Woonsocket as *All For the Union*. This book is a publication of the fair copy of Rhodes' diary which he recopied after the war, and differs in some places from his field journal kept during the war, especially in his opinions of the Union high command. The book was not widely known until Rhodes' neighbor in New Hampshire, Ken Burns bought a copy. Burns used Elisha Hunt Rhodes as the archetypical Union soldier in his 1990 series *The Civil War*. *All For the Union* was republished in paperback by Random House, selling tens of thousands of copies, and becoming the most widely read book about Rhode Island and the Civil War.

In the early 1990s, Kris VanDenBossche, an antiques dealer from Hopkinton formed the Rhode Island Historical Document Transcription Project. He traveled the state seeking out documents and photographs for inclusion in a project sponsored by the Rhode Island Council of the Humanities. VanDenBossche gathered hundreds of letters and transcribed them for publication. His book, *Pleas Excuse All Bad Writing* was distributed to every library in Rhode Island and not made available for sale to the

---

[10] Harold R. Barker, *History of the Rhode Island Combat Units in the Civil War (1861-1865)*. Providence: NP, 1964. Harold R. Barker Papers, Rhode Island Historical Society and Benefit Street Arsenal, Providence, RI.

general public. A companion volume, *Write Soon and Give Me All The News* is found at the Rhode Island Historical Society. These books are two of the best and most available sources of letters written by Rhode Island soldiers.[11]

In 1996 Butternut & Blue, a Maryland based publisher of Civil War books reissued the histories of the First Rhode Island Cavalry and Battery B, First Rhode Island Light Artillery as part of their Army of the Potomac Series. These two republications featured an extensive introduction about both units written by Robert Durwood Madison, a native Rhode Islander and then professor of history at the United States Naval Academy. With the advent of newer, cheaper, publishing technologies, companies such as Higginson Books in Salem, Massachusetts began to reissue reprints of regimental histories. Previously only available at libraries or for hefty sums from rare book dealers, these reprints made the regimental histories available to the public again. With the emergence of a renewed interest in the Civil War beginning in the late 1980s and the founding of the Rhode Island Civil War Round Table, reenacting groups such as Battery B and the Second Rhode Island, as well as a surge of membership in the Rhode Island Sons of Union Veterans, there was a renewed interest in the history of Rhode Island and the Civil War era, which led to spate of new publications.

Perhaps the greatest contribution to the historiography of Rhode Island and the Civil War era has been made by Robert Grandchamp. A twelfth generation Rhode Islander, Grandchamp, at an early age discovered that his third great uncle, Alfred Sheldon Knight had served and died in the service as a member of Company C, Seventh Rhode Island Volunteers. Inspired by his ancestor's service, he took an active interest in the overall history of Rhode Island and the Civil War in high school that eventually took him to Rhode Island College where he earned an M.A. in American history. Grandchamp believed firmly in conducting in-

---

[11] *Standard Times,* April 8, 1992. *Westerly Sun,* May 23, 1993. *Westerly Sun,* August 2, 1992.

depth, primary research on the Civil War by visiting every historical society, archive, and library in the state, as well as visiting nearly every Civil War era graveyard in Rhode Island. Furthermore, he has traveled the country, visiting museums, libraries, and battlefields gathering material from out of state sources on Rhode Island participation. In addition, he actively collected and continues to collect books, artifacts, and manuscript material on Rhode Island military history.

In his nearly twenty years of research, Grandchamp has come to be widely considered as the nation's foremost authority on Rhode Island military history. He is often consulted by the Rhode Island National Guard, the Varnum Continentals, Kentish Guards, and other organizations for his expertise in military history. During his college years, from 2008-2010 he was the lead researcher and writer on a history of the Providence Marine Corps of Artillery and the 103rd Field Artillery of the Rhode Island National Guard. Grandchamp served as a National Park Ranger at Harpers Ferry and Shenandoah. This experience led to many contacts in the historical community that can be tapped as needed. In 2012, Robert researched and led a program as part of Rhode Island Day at Antietam National Battlefield.

Robert's work has been published in a wide variety of national and local magazines and journals. He is a frequent contributor to *Rhode Island Roots,* published by the Rhode Island Genealogical Society. Furthermore, in 2017 he published a controversial article in *America's Civil War* magazine that established that Sullivan Ballou did not write the famous last letter made famous in Ken Burns' *Civil War* series. In addition, he has authored a dozen books for which he received letters of commendation from Governor Lincoln Chaffee and Mayor Angel Tavares of Providence. In addition, he became the first civilian recipient of the Order of St. Barbara from the Rhode Island National Guard for his contributions to the history of the Rhode Island artillery community. Among Grandchamp's writings are regimental histories of the Seventh Rhode Island Volunteers and Battery G, First Rhode Island Light Artillery. He has edited the correspondence of several Rhode Island soldiers, co-authored a bicentennial history of the Providence Marine Corps of Artillery, and wrote the popular book, *Rhode Island and the Civil War: Voices from the Ocean State.*

In addition to Robert Grandchamp's work, the Sesquicentennial of the Civil War also saw several other publications. Although widely known as a Lincoln scholar, Judge Frank Williams, the chair of the state committee for the Sesquicentennial edited a book about the contributions of those Rhode Islanders who remained at home during the war. Frank Grzyb, a Vietnam veteran and retired government employee wrote *Hidden History of Rhode Island and the Civil War* and *Rhode Island's Civil War Hospital: Life and Death at Portsmouth Grove.* Most recently the East Providence Historical Society released *All Quiet on the Rappahannock Tonight,* which is a compilation of the letters of Lieutenant Peter Hunt of Battery A who was mortally wounded at Cold Harbor.

Unfortunately, the future does not appear bright for continued publications about Rhode Island and the Civil War. While the veterans who took part in the conflict wanted their story told and often wrote about it through the publications of the Soldiers and Sailors Historical Society, or in state sponsored regimental histories, current scholarship in the field is limited to two active participants, while academia often does not view the study of Civil War military history in the best light.

The Civil War Sesquicentennial commemorated from 2011-2015 was a litmus test for Rhode Island that unfortunately the state failed at. While other states such as Virginia, South Carolina, Maine, and notably Connecticut supported and funded commissions to organize sesquicentennial events and publications, Rhode Island only organized a group in February 2011. Led by noted Lincoln scholar and retired Chief Justice Frank Williams, the twenty-seven-member commissioned, comprised of Rhode Islanders from a wide array of backgrounds published a lofty mission statement:

The Commission and its advisory council will explore and publicize this important history – military, political, and cultural – in a myriad of ways during the years 2011 through 2015. We will support projects to restore Civil War monuments and to digitize Civil War related data; we will endorse reenactments and exhibits, expand this website, and produce publications; and we will devote much energy to the education of our citizens – especially students – about this crucial era of our history. The volunteer efforts of the Commission, its advisory council, supportive educators, and Rhode Island citizens in general – all without remuneration – will strive to meet these goals.

Unfortunately, few, if any of these goals were met. While a website was created by the commission and they did include some images of Rhode Island soldiers, and some events were listed, the website did not accomplish much, in comparison to neighboring Connecticut which frequently updated with events taking place all through the Nutmeg State. The twenty-seven-member committee proved to be unwieldly, while the Rhode Island General Assembly did not fund the commission's work; instead they had to rely on donations to remain active.

In April 2011, a group of Rhode Islanders met at the Benefit Street Arsenal to commemorate 150 years since the Providence Marine Corps of Artillery left the building as one of the first groups of northern militia to respond to Lincoln's call for volunteers. Four years later, another ceremony was held at the arsenal to commemorate the end of the war and to dedicate a plaque to the seven soldiers of Battery G who earned the Medal of Honor at Petersburg on April 2, 1865. With the exception of the annual Fort Adams reenactment, and Rhode Island Day at Antietam National Battlefield, neither event being sponsored by the commission, few events transpired in Rhode Island during the sesquicentennial.

While Connecticut sponsored an official sesquicentennial history of Nutmeg State participation, Rhode Island did not.

Rather, the Rhode Island Sesquicentennial Commission secured a small grant to publish *The Rhode Island Homefront in the Civil War Era,* a compilation of essays regarding economic, social, and political events in Rhode Island. Sam Simons published a well-received series of bi-weekly articles in *The Westerly Sun* from 2012-2013, but even these were only read locally in South County. A planned one-day symposium in April 2014 was canceled due to lack of pre-registration. Unfortunately, in the end, the Civil War Sesquicentennial was a failure in Rhode Island and did not generate the interest in the conflict that was created in other states.

Why, unlike other states, is the Civil War often placed on the backburner in Rhode Island? In Maine, one can walk into the stately home of war hero General Joshua Lawrence Chamberlain; in Connecticut one can visit the restored Grand Army of the Republic Hall in Rockville, now home to the New England Civil War Museum. Lebanon, New Hampshire also boasts a restored GAR Hall, while a visitor can drive to many historical sites in Vermont, including the American Precision Museum in Windsor which was originally a musket manufacturing center. In Rhode Island, with the exception of Fort Adams and the Westerly Public Library, once a GAR Hall, few, if any tangible sites remain in Rhode Island relating to the Civil War. Furthermore, much of the state's vast history is stored away in archival boxes at Brown University, the Rhode Island Historical Society, and the Rhode Island State Archives. With the exception of the magnificent Varnum Continentals collection in East Greenwich, there is not a major museum in the state dedicated to Rhode Island's rich military history.

There are several major reasons why Rhode Island Civil War history is not front and center. Firstly, Rhode Island does not have a statewide history museum to tell the story of the state's past. The proposed Heritage Harbor Museum in Providence never came to fruition. Local historical societies, while meaning well, often lack in trained personnel. Few have the resources they need. In addition, there is not a dedicated facility to host the rich and vast state archives. Rather, the archives are held in a cluttered, risk prone building in the middle of downtown Providence, instead of in a dedicated facility like every other New England state.

Rhode Island is very much a community of continued immigration from around the world. As each new ethnic group comes into Rhode Island, they do not look to the deeds of the past. The Irish and Quebecois were active participants in the Civil War experience in Rhode Island, however as they were supplemented by the Italians, in turn by Latinos and East Asians. Each new group, while bringing much and contributing to the vitality of Rhode Island, has not embraced the rich historical past of Rhode Island. One only need to look at the Soldiers and Sailors Monument in Providence to understand this. The monument is frequently covered in pigeon excrement, while vagabonds sleep, and transients sit wild eyed on this sacred place to commemorate Rhode Islanders who gave "the last full measure of devotion."

In addition, Rhode Island history is not, for the most part, an academic discipline. With the retirement of Patrick Conley from Providence College, and Stanley Lemons from Rhode Island College, the state lost two of the best academics in the field of Rhode Island history that were not replaced with equal peers in the field. Another bright light was lost in 2017 when Albert Klyberg, former head of the Rhode Island Historical Society, and one of the state's foremost champions of history died. While Rhode Island College, the University of Rhode Island, and others teach Rhode Island history classes, they are general survey courses, not in-depth studies. Also inhibiting is the lack of an academic press attached to a university or college in Rhode Island publishing books about the rich history of the state. When academics do study Rhode Island history it is largely the colonial period, or Rhode Island's notorious involvement in the Triangle Trade. Even the Fourteenth Rhode Island Heavy Artillery, a black regiment, has not received the academic treatment of the neighboring Fifty-Fourth Massachusetts. A lack of education about Rhode Island history, coupled with a disregard of the state's history have all contributed to Rhode Island Civil War history being neglected.

In conclusion, the history of Rhode Island and the Civil War must continue to be studied. The Civil War was and remains the defining moment in American history. Rhode Islanders left an indelible mark on the battlefield and in the pages of the history they wrote. It waits to be seen if future generations will pick up the pen and continue writing about the noble deeds they achieved.

Chapter Ten:

Ocean State Confederates

Before the Civil War, Newport was a favorite vacation destination for southerners to escape the hot summers of their plantations. While Rhode Island had gradually ended slavery after the Revolution, Southerners, with the passage of slavery protection laws (which was one of many catalysts leading to the war) could freely take their slaves with them to Rhode Island. Rhode Island's most famous son of the time, Nathanael Greene had moved to Georgia after the Revolution, owned slaves, and was buried in Savannah. Many Rhode Islanders had family members in the South. In addition, Brown University was a popular educational institute for Southerners, some of whom joined the Confederate service. Furthermore, many mills in Rhode Island depended on the availability of cheap cotton to manufacture their goods. The Rodman mills of South Kingstown were well known for their "slave cloth," coarse fabric sold to plantation owners to outfit their slaves with. In essence, the Ocean State had a deep connection to the South.[1]

Surprisingly, a handful of Rhode Islanders fought *for* the Confederacy in support of slavery and states' rights. Samuel Newell of Pawtucket was one of them. He had traveled to Alabama before the war and worked on a railroad near Montgomery. When the Civil War broke out in April 1861, he wanted to return to Rhode Island and boarded a train for New York. The train stopped in Richmond, Virginia, where Newell was

---

[1] Charles Hoffman and Tess Hoffman, *North By South: The Two Lives of Richard James Arnold*. (Athens: University of Georgia Press, 1988), 6-10: 211-222. Robert Hudson George, *Brown University on the Eve of the Civil War; Brunonians in Confederate Ranks, 1861-1865*. (Providence: Brown University, 1965), 19-34.

robbed of his money and thrown in jail. After four months in prison he was offered his freedom if he joined the Confederate Army. Enlisting in the Ashland Virginia Artillery, Newell served during the Seven Days Battles in the summer of 1862 and at Second Manassas. He deserted in September 1862 during the Maryland Campaign. He traveled to Greencastle, Pennsylvania where ironically the first Union troops he encountered, the Seventh Squadron of Rhode Island Cavalry, were commanded by a neighbor from Pawtucket. In an interview with a local paper, Newell spoke of the terrible, ragged condition of the Rebel Army, the poor food they ate, and the fact that sixty-year-old men were being pressed into service. The *Providence Evening Press* concluded, "Mr. N seems to be extremely happy in having effected his escape from rebeldom."[2]

Other Rhode Islanders who fought for the South were the sons of Richard Arnold, a wealthy planter who originally hailed from Providence and who owned plantations in Georgia. During one battle, Elisha Hunt Rhodes of the Second Rhode Island Volunteers found himself facing James R. Sheldon of Georgia, a former resident of Pawtuxet, whom Rhodes called "my old schoolmate and neighbor." Private Henry Augustus Middleton was born in South Carolina in 1829; his parents were from Newport, Rhode Island. He was mortally wounded at First Bull Run, fighting not far from where Newporter Theodore Wheaton King of the First Rhode Island Detached Militia was mortally wounded. The Civil War truly was brother against brother. A handful called the Ocean State home in the decades after the conflict and at least five are known to be buried here: these are their stories.[3]

Samuel Postlethwaite, born April 6, 1833 in Mississippi is the most famous of the Ocean State Rebels. After reading a state by state guide to Civil War sites in 1990, Les Rolston, a Warwick

---

[2] *Providence Evening Press,* September 26, 1862.
[3] Hoffman and Hoffman, *North by South,* 233-244. Elisha Hunt Rhodes, *All for the Union: The Civil War Diary & Letters of Elisha Hunt Rhodes.* Edited by Robert H. Rhodes. (Woonsocket: Andrew Mowbray, 1985), 181. David King to William Porcher, July 29, 1861, Southern Historical Collection, University of North Carolina, Chapel Hill, North Carolina.

building inspector and amateur historian was intrigued by the story of a Confederate soldier buried in Greenwood Cemetery in Coventry. He began doing research and found the remarkable story of Postlethwaite who served in Company D of the Twenty-First Mississippi during the war.

Wounded at Malvern Hill in 1862, Postlethwaite suffered terribly from his war wounds, and developed tuberculosis. After the conflict, his sister married into the prominent Greene family in Coventry, Rhode Island, and Samuel went north in 1875 to seek relief from his war wounds. He died on August 20, 1876 and was buried in Greenwood Cemetery. In 1994, Rolston and several descendants of the family placed a government issued grave marker of Postlethwaite's otherwise unmarked grave. The grave is the site of a Confederate Memorial Day ceremony each spring.[4]

Rolston was honored by several historical groups for his efforts, and later published the book, *Lost Soul: A Confederate Soldier in New England.* A popular local history book, *Lost Soul* has gone through several editions and remains in print as a popular study of the war. In his 2013 book, *Hidden History of Rhode Island and the Civil War,* Frank Grzyb issued a challenge, "According to Rolston, Postlethwaite is the only known Confederate buried in Rhode Island. No one has yet come forward to prove otherwise." This writer loves a challenge and has now established several more known Confederate burials in Rhode Island.[5]

Anyone who saw the 1993 movie *Gettysburg* easily recalls the powerful performance of actor Richard Jordan as Brigadier General Lewis Addison Armistead. Jordan accurately played Armistead as a hardened West Pointer and Mexican War hero who resigned at the start of the war to join the Confederacy. Armistead struggled with his conscious on the night of July 2, 1863 when he

---

[4] For more on Postlethwaite, refer to Les Rolston's *Lost Soul: A Confederate Soldier in New England.* (Buena Vista, VA: Mariner Publishing, 2007)

[5] Frank Grzyb, *Hidden History of Rhode Island and the Civil War.* (Charleston, SC: History Press, 2013), 184-186.

realized the next day he would have to lead his men into battle against his best friend, Union Second Corps commander General Winfield Scott Hancock. In the end, Armistead bravely led his troops into action at Pickett's Charge where he was mortally wounded and died two days later. For many viewers, the feeling of Armistead is that he is an old bachelor whose entire life was spent in the military. Despite this perspective, General Armistead left a son who called Rhode Island home.[6]

Walker Keith Armistead was the son of Lewis Addison Armistead and his first wife Cecelia Lee Love. He was born on December 11, 1844 in Dallas County, Alabama. He was named after his grandfather, who had graduated from West Point in 1803 and later became chief engineer of the United States Army. During the Civil War, Armistead served as an aide de camp on his father's staff and was with him at Gettysburg, but as he was not listed as killed or wounded more than likely did not follow his father into action at Pickett's Charge. He later was a private in Company A of the Sixth Virginia Cavalry, often acting as a staff courier. Armistead was wounded on June 29, 1864. While it has been written that Armistead was with the Confederate cause "to the end," his name is not listed among the parolees of the Army of Northern Virginia who surrendered at Appomattox.[7]

After the "close of the late Rebellion," in 1871, Armistead married Julia Webster Appleton, the granddaughter of legendary statesman Daniel Webster. Together they had three sons, Walker Keith who died in 1890 while on a hunting trip in Maine, and Daniel Webster who lived until 1949 and later moved to Pennsylvania. A third son, Lewis Addison, was born in 1872. He spent much of his life in Newport and served in the Spanish-American War and First World War; he died in 1933.[8]

---

[6] Refer to Wayne E. Motts, *"Trust in God and Fear Nothing:" Gen. Lewis A. Armistead, CSA.* (Gettysburg: Farnsworth House, 1994)
[7] Confederate Compiled Military Service Records, Virginia, Walker Keith Armistead, Sixth Cavalry, National Archives. Index of Confederate Paroles issued April 9-12, 1865, Appomattox National Historical Park, Appomattox Court House, Virginia.
[8] *Newport Mercury,* October 6, 1933.

After his service in the Confederate Army, Armistead and his family moved to New Jersey, but in 1882 they built a residence of Gibbs Avenue in Newport. Here he worked as a court reporter and was known as an "expert stenographer." In addition, Armistead served as president of the Society for the Prevention of Cruelty to Animals in Boston. Armistead died at his residence in Newport on March 28, 1898 and is buried at St. Columba's Cemetery in Middletown.[9]

Island Cemetery in Newport is one of my favorite places to explore. As a historian, I use cemeteries as an invaluable primary resource, often finding genealogical data and other information found nowhere else. Except for Swan Point and North Burial Ground in Providence, no Rhode Island cemetery contains as many famous characters of Rhode Island's past as does Island Cemetery. In 2009, while wandering through the rows of stones, I made a remarkable discovery. In a back corner of Island Cemetery, right along a fence line is the grave of Union Major General Gouverneur Kemble Warren, a former engineer and corps commander, Warren discovered the threat to the Union left at Gettysburg and hurried troops to Little Round Top to save the day for the Army of the Potomac. He died in Newport in 1882. Not far from Warren's grave, I saw a large, rather unremarkable blue-gray slate stone with the name Robert Cooper engraved upon it. Only really interested in studying the graves of Civil War soldiers, I was about to walk by when my mouth dropped. Cooper was a Civil War soldier! Underneath his name was the engraving "Co. B 7th Va." He was a Confederate soldier.

Robert Cooper was born in Virginia in 1845. He enlisted as a private in Company B of the Seventh Virginia Infantry on March 1, 1864. The Seventh Virginia had been slaughtered during Pickett's Charge at Gettysburg, as such it spent the early spring of

---

[9] Walker Keith Armistead, 1844-1896, http://www.findagrave.com/cgi bin/fg.cgi?page=gr&GSln=armistead&GSfn=walker&GSmn=keith+&G Sbyrel=all&GSdyrel=all&GSob=n&GRid=8684554&df=all&, accessed November 20, 2016.

1864 recovering near Drewry's Bluff, Virginia as part of Pickett's Division, thus missing the carnage of the Wilderness and Spotsylvania Court House. Cooper was present throughout the summer of 1864 with his company and was present at the Battle of Drewry's Bluff and other actions as part of the Bermuda Hundred and Petersburg Campaigns. Cooper was sick in a hospital in Richmond on April 3, 1865 when the city fell to Union forces. He was turned over to the provost marshal and allowed to go home on May 28, 1865.[10]

After the war, Robert married Virginia and at an unknown time moved to Newport. He was in the city by 1879, as their first-born child is buried in Island Cemetery, two more children Harry and Hattie followed, but they also died in childhood; Virginia followed in 1916. Private Robert Cooper died in Newport in 1926 at the age of eighty-one. As proud of his service in the Army of Northern Virginia, as the men who served in Rhode Island units buried around him, Cooper had his military service engraved on his stone for eternity.[11]

A fourth confirmed Confederate soldier from Rhode Island is Dr. William Dixon Horton. He served as an assistant surgeon in the Tenth Tennessee Infantry. Horton was born in Nashville on August 29, 1835. He attended the University of Nashville for his medical degree and obtained his doctorate in 1859. Horton joined the Tenth Tennessee as its assistant surgeon in the spring of 1861 and by December 1861 was serving at Fort Henry on the Tennessee River. When the fort fell to Union forces under Ulysses S. Grant on February 6, 1862, Horton was captured. Like most medical personnel however, he was paroled to treat the wounded. Oftentimes Confederate records are sketchy at best, but

---

[10] Confederate Compiled Military Service Records, Virginia, Seventh Infantry, Robert Cooper, National Archives.
[11] Robert Cooper, 1845-1926, http://www.findagrave.com/cgibin/fg.cgi?page=gr&GSln=cooper&GSfn=robert&GSbyrel=all&GSdy=1926&GSdyrel=in&GSob=n&GRid=21594181&df=all&, accessed November 20, 2016.

as far as the record indicates, Horton took no further part in the conflict.[12]

In 1870, he was living in Memphis as the "City Inspector." In 1875, he was residing back in Nashville and filed a U.S. patent for "Improvement in Umbrellas." By 1880, Dr. Horton had moved to New England and resided in Providence, working as a "physician." He was a boarder and resided with his wife Annie, and daughter Edith.[13]

Horton later moved to Arlington, Massachusetts and on April 28, 1892 sailed with his wife to Europe. He intended a "temporary sojourn" in Bern, Switzerland, but it turned out to last for several decades; there is no further evidence of Horton residing in Providence after the 1880 census. His wife Annie died in Bern in 1914. After the death of his wife, and with his daughter residing in London, he returned to Providence. Dr. Horton died in Providence in 1918. Why the city that he only resided in for a short time was chosen as his final resting place is unknown. His grave in North Burial Ground in Providence is marked by a large Catholic cross.[14]

The Ocean State Confederate who left behind the greatest written record is Captain Richard Washington Corbin who served as a staff officer in the Army of Northern Virginia during the

---

[12] William D. Horton, "An Inaugural Dissertation on the Education of a Physician," Vanderbilt University Archives, Nashville, Tennessee. Confederate Compiled Military Service Records, Tennessee, Tenth Infantry, William Dixon Horton, National Archives.
[13] 1870 U.S. Census, Memphis, Tennessee, National Archives. William D. Horton, Improvement in Umbrellas. U.S. Patent 161962, filed February 25, 1875, and issued April 13, 1875. 1880 U.S. Census, Providence, RI.
[14] William Dixon Horton, Emergency Passport Application, July 30, 1898, Emergency Passport Applications (Issued Abroad), 1877-1907; Roll #: 54; Volume #: Volume 106: Switzerland, National Archives. William Dixon Horton, 1835-1918, http://www.findagrave.com/cgi-bin/fg.cgi?page=gr&GSln=horton&GSfn=william+&GSmn=dixon&GSb yrel=all&GSdyrel=in&GSob=n&GRid=18618596&df=all&, accessed November 20, 2016.

Siege of Petersburg. Corbin was the author of the book *Letters of a Confederate Officer to His Family in Europe During the Last Year of the War of Secession.* This book provides a fantastic view of the last months of Lee's Army on the Petersburg siege line.

Corbin was born in Paris, France, the son of Virginia parents. Raised in France, he went to England in 1864 and volunteered for Confederate service. After a harrowing trip from Europe through Bermuda on a blockade runner, Corbin made it to Virginia, where he served as an aide on the staff of Major General Charles W. Field. Corbin saw service on the front lines, and wrote detailed letters to his family back in Paris that were later published. Captain Corbin remained with General Field to the end and surrendered at Appomattox.

With the war over, Corbin "overcame his antipathy for at least one Yankee." He married Bessie Rhodes of Providence and moved back to France. The couple had two boys. With the start of World War, I in 1914, an aged Corbin moved with his wife to Newport, Rhode Island where he spent his final years. Corbin died on February 22, 1922 and is interred at Island Cemetery in Newport. As is typical of most New England Confederates, his stone is unadorned with any Confederate device.[15]

One Rebel who spent a large amount of time in Rhode Island is John Shea; however, he is buried on the other side of the Pawcatuck River, in Connecticut. He was born in County Kerry Ireland in 1840 and by the outbreak of the Civil War was residing in Nashville. He joined Company C of the Tenth Tennessee Infantry, which served as part of the Army of the Tennessee. A post-war newspaper article claimed that Shea "served with valor throughout the conflict." His service file however indicates that he was captured at Fort Donelson in February 1862. He took the oath of allegiance to the United States on August 30, 1862, was released from prison at Camp Douglas, Illinois. He saw no further service. He moved to New Haven, Connecticut and by 1878 had

---

[15] Richard W. Corbin, *Letters of a Confederate Officer to His Family in Europe During the Last Year of the War of Secession.* (Baltimore: Butternut & Blue, 1993)

settled in Pawcatuck. Shea worked as a "quarry man" in the Westerly granite industry and also as a "fish peddler." Shea died in 1916 after raising four children; he is buried in St. Michael's Cemetery in Pawcatuck. In 1938, the United Daughters of the Confederacy sent a grave marker and Confederate battle flag to be placed on his grave. The local *Westerly Sun* declared Shea "the only Confederate veteran buried in New London or Washington Counties, as far as is known."[16]

Is there a possibility of additional Confederates being buried in Rhode Island: Absolutely. Confederate prisoners were housed at Portsmouth Grove Hospital on Aquidneck Island. Men who took the oath of allegiance to the United States were allowed to be released from prison. A local story abounds in Jamestown of a Confederate soldier falling in love with a local nurse from the hospital, taking the oath, and eventually becoming a farmer on Conanicut Island; his identity is unknown.[17]

Episcopal Bishop of Rhode Island, Thomas M. Clark was a frequent visitor to Portsmouth Grove Hospital during the war. One-day Clark recalled visiting the cemetery at Portsmouth Grove.

> I was looking one day upon the little cemetery where the bodies of those who had died were buried, and I observed that a certain number of the graves were adorned with three large quahog shells, gathered on the neighboring shore, while the other graves were only ornamented with one shell. I asked the veteran who had charge of the place what this meant, and he replied, "Them graves with only one shell are the Confederates," and I afterward found that he supposed himself to have had some special grievance

---

[16] Confederate Compiled Military Service Records, Tennessee, Tenth Infantry, John Shea, National Archives. Cemetery Records, St. Michael's Catholic Cemetery, Pawcatuck, Connecticut. *Westerly Sun,* May 26, 1938.
[17] Frank Grzyb, *Rhode Island's Civil War Hospital: Life and Death at Portsmouth Grove, 1862-1865.* (Jefferson, NC: McFarland, 2012), 54: 170.

and relived his mind by making this somewhat invidious distinction.

Bishop Clark also recalled that the Confederates "went about with freedom," and spent most of their spare time fishing in Narragansett Bay. Although anxious to return to their homes in the South, no escapes were reported in local papers. Clark later arranged for some Confederates to be returned to New Orleans after their treatment at the hospital.[18]

After the war these veterans traveled all over the world; indeed, some are buried in Europe, New Zealand, Japan, and Australia. One interesting fact comes from a 1912 booklet, *Report of Commissioner for Marking Confederate Graves.* "One Confederate prisoner of war died at Providence, R.I. but his remains were later removed to Cypress Hills National Cemetery, Brooklyn, N.Y." An 1874 Decoration Day speech alluded to a Confederate burial in the Fort Adams Cemetery in Newport, but no confirmation has yet to be made.[19]

As the losing side in a bitter war, unlike nearly every Union veteran, few Confederate veterans who moved to New England, with the notable exception of Robert Cooper, listed their military service upon their gravestone. Without such a feature, it is nearly impossible to distinguish Confederate graves from others. None of the known graves has distinguishing grave devices typically found on graves in the South, and none, with the occasional exception of Samuel Postlethwaite is marked with a Confederate flag. Doubtless additional Rebels rest under the rocky soil of Rhode Island, some in unmarked graves.

Although Rhode Island was staunchly pro-Union, some Rhode Islanders did fight for the Confederacy, while a few were

---

[18] Thomas M. Clark, *Reminiscences.* (New York: Thomas Whittaker, 1895), 148-149.
[19] *Report of Commissioner for Marking Confederate Graves.* (Washington, DC: Government Printing Office, 1912), 4 *Newport Daily News,* June 1, 1874.

marked to spend eternity in the Ocean State. Several local Civil War reenacting units portray members of the Confederate army. The South Kingstown High School sports teams are known as the Rebels. The team used to fly the Confederate battle flag and had a Confederate soldier for a mascot; indeed, one yearbook from the 1970s featured an Army of Northern Virginia battle flag on the cover. In today's politically fueled climate, the debate continues to rage in that town about changing the name of the team to something else. During the eighteenth-century Rhode Island was one of the largest importers of slaves into the colonies. From 1861-1865 thousands of young Rhode Islanders went south to free the slave and reunite the United States as soldiers of the Union. Other Rhode Islanders fought to preserve slavery in a divided nation. It is a part of Rhode Island history that should not be forgotten.

Chapter Eleven:

"They have just brought one more:"

Two Letters from Bethesda Church

In the spring and summer of 1864, the Union Army of the Potomac suffered over 50,000 casualties as they conducted the Overland Campaign to finally destroy Lee's Army of Northern Virginia. In places that have long since entered the American lexicon such as the Wilderness, Spotsylvania Court House, North Anna River, Totopotomy, Cold Harbor, Bethesda Church, Haw's Shop, Petersburg, the Crater, and Poplar Spring Church, the Union forces tried desperately to outmaneuver Lee and capture Richmond. Finally, by mid-June they trapped the Confederates at Petersburg, which led to a nine-month siege, and the eventual surrender of the Army of Northern Virginia.

The Seventh Rhode Island Volunteers was part of these actions. Raised in the summer of 1862, the Seventh had been bloodied at Fredericksburg in December 1862, losing forty percent of its strength. In the spring of 1863, they transferred to the Western Theatre, performing garrison duty in Kentucky and then being sent to Mississippi in June. For two months, the Rhode Islanders slogged through the swamps of Mississippi, seeing action at Vicksburg and Jackson. The regiment returned to Kentucky in late August a mere shell of itself, with fewer than 100 men able to perform any duty. Diseases such as typhoid, dysentery, malaria, and Yazoo Fever killed over fifty Rhode Islanders, and led to the discharge of many others. After performing duty in rural Kentucky in the winter of 1863, while regaining the strength of the regiment, the Seventh and its parent organization, the Ninth Corps returned to Annapolis, Maryland in April 1864 in time to take part in Grant's Overland Campaign.[1]

When the Seventh left Annapolis in late April, the regiment had twenty officers and 264 "muskets" or enlisted men present for duty. General Ulysses S. Grant, now in command of all Union forces ordered his men to attack Lee in the thickets of the Wilderness on May 5-6, 1864. The battle was a draw, but unlike other Union commanders, Grant did not retreat, rather he ordered his men south towards Spotsylvania. Fortunately, the Seventh was in reserve at the Wilderness, losing only four men wounded. A week later however, the Seventh's luck ran out. Fighting for a week straight in the sanguine moonscape of Spotsylvania Court House, including the horrific May 12, 1864 at the Bloody Angle, where the two sides fought in hand to hand combat for hours in the pouring rain. The regiment was also heavily engaged on May 18, when they were ordered to attack a fortified position alone, and without other support. From May 12-May 18, 1864, the Seventh lost nineteen men killed in action and fifty-six wounded. Worse was to come.[2]

On May 23, the Seventh was under fire again at the North Anna River, losing six men, including two killed in action, among them Sergeant Samuel F. Simpson of Company I, the regimental color bearer.[3] Finally by late May, Grant had outmaneuvered Lee and was in a position to finally capture Richmond and end the war. Lee hurried south and threw up a line of impregnable defenses at

---

[1] William P. Hopkins, *The Seventh Regiment Rhode Island Volunteers in the Civil War, 1862-1865*. (Providence: Snow & Farnum, 1903), 1-51.
[2] George A. Spencer to Parents, June 12, 1864, author's collection. Seventh Rhode Island Volunteers, Descriptive Book, Rhode Island State Archives, Providence, RI. For specifics on the Wilderness and Spotsylvania, refer to Gordon C. Rhea, *The Battle of the Wilderness: May 5-6, 1864*. (Baton Rouge: Louisiana State University Press, 1994) and Gordon C. Rhea, *The Battles for Spotsylvania Court House and the Road to Yellow Tavern, May 7-12, 1864*. (Baton Rouge: Louisiana State University Press, 1997).
[3] Gordon C. Rhea, *To the North Anna River: Grant and Lee, May 13-25, 1864*. (Baton Rouge: Louisiana State University Press, 2000)

Cold Harbor, a small crossroads only six miles from Richmond. The soldiers in the Army of the Potomac were so close to the city, they could hear the church bells ringing. Grant ordered an initial assault on June 1, 1864 which was beaten back with heavy loss. Two days later, the Union commander ordered an all-out assault on Lee's lines, determined to finally capture Richmond and end the war. In ten minutes of slaughter, nearly 5,000 Union soldiers were killed or wounded. General Grant later wrote in his memoirs, "I have always regretted that the last assault on Cold Harbor was ever made. No advantage whatever was gained to compensate for the heavy losses we sustained."[4]

At seven on the morning of June 3, 1864 there were fewer than 150 officers and men left in the Seventh Rhode Island to make the charge. Ordered to assault at a place called Bethesda Church, the Seventh was stationed on the extreme right flank of the Army of the Potomac, and assaulted north of where the main Union attack took place. The Seventh's orders took led them straight into a heavily fortified position held by two brigades of North Carolinians. Drummer William P. Hopkins of Company D recalled, "Forward we went through an underbrush swamp so dense it was impossible to maintain line formation." The mud was so thick it pulled the boots off some of the men. The Seventh crossed Matadequin Creek under heavy fire from a Virginia battery. These men were veterans, they would not run, but pushed forward.[5]

The North Carolinians to their front opened a murderous fire on the Seventh. Company F, comprised of men from North Kingstown and Exeter took the brunt of the fire, losing five dead and three wounded out of only fourteen men in line that morning. Corporal Nathan B. Lewis, a twenty-one-year-old former teacher from Exeter, destined to become a judge in South County took command of the shattered force as the Seventh tried to maintain their position under "a terrible fire," as one Seventh officer wrote.

---

[4] For the Battle of Cold Harbor, refer to Gordon C. Rhea, *Cold Harbor: Grant and Lee: May 26-June 3, 1864.* (Baton Rouge: University of Louisiana Press, 2002).
[5] Hopkins, *Seventh Rhode Island,* 184-186.

As men were shot, they fell into the thick mud, as the musicians worked feverishly to drag the wounded to the surgeons on the other side of the creek, while the officers screamed at the top of their lungs for the men to load and fire; each soldier quickly went through the sixty rounds he was carrying, going into the cartridge boxes of the dead and wounded to find additional ammunition.[6]

The Rhode Islanders fought to within sixty yards of the Confederate line before they halted and worked like men possessed to dig a line of entrenchments, using bayonets, tin cups, and their bare hands to throw up a line of crude fortifications. Private Jared J. Potter, a member of Company G from Richmond, Rhode Island wrote. "We charged the swamp + drove them from one line of works + put up works in front of their second line we lost heavy." Unable to retreat or push forward, the Rhode Islanders and the rest of their brigade dug in. At 3:00 that afternoon, General Ambrose Burnside, the commander of the Ninth Corps ordered his men to attack again, but the orders were canceled by Grant. This no doubt saved the lives of many members of the Seventh. The regiment came under sniper fire from Confederates in the trees to the front. After inflicting several casualties on the Seventh, a number of men formed a party who tracked the sniper. Drummer Hopkins recalled, "Just as his head and rifle came in sight as he was preparing for another shot, a number of men fired simultaneously. There was no more sharpshooting from that angle." During the night, the Confederates evacuated their position, allowing the Seventh to wander into the Rebel entrenchments on June 4. Private William O. Harrington of Foster who served in Company K recorded, "The fight has been very heavy." [7]

The Seventh Rhode Island again paid dearly for its reputation as a hard fighting, dependable regiment at Bethesda

[6] Rhea, Cold Harbor, 369-377. *Providence Journal,* June 20, 1864.
[7] Rhea, Cold Harbor, 369-377. Hopkins, *Seventh Rhode Island,* 184-188. Jared J. Potter, diary, June 3, 1864, University of Rhode Island Special Collections, South Kingstown, RI. William O. Harrington to Eunice Harrington, June 4, 1864, North Scituate Public Library, North Scituate, RI.

Church. Roughly 150 men went into action on the morning of June 3, 1864 of this one-third were killed or wounded, sixteen men died and another 29 were wounded on June 3. In all, the Seventh lost forty-nine killed in action or mortally wounded, as well as 152 wounded, and several captured in the Overland Campaign. By mid-June 1864 when the Seventh arrived at Petersburg only seventy-five men remained of the 960 that had left Rhode Island in September 1862. Company H, recruited in Warwick and East Greenwich mustered only one man present for duty. William P. Hopkins remembered, "It was about this time when the ranks were so reduced there seemed to be no Seventh Regiment."[8]

Private Harrington of Foster perhaps best summed up the Seventh's losses. "I dont know how many we have lost in all." The regiment was pulled off the line and assigned to the engineer corps to perform rear-echelon duty, while they rebuilt their strength from those wounded men able to return to the regiment, men returning from extended duty elsewhere, as well as the eventual consolidation of the Fourth and Seventh Rhode Island Regiments in October 1864.[9]

The author of these letters is Private George A. Spencer of Company I. The East Bay company of the Seventh, Company I included a platoon of men from Bristol and one from Newport. George A. Spencer was the son of Edward and Alice (Rice) Spencer. He was born in Smithfield, Rhode Island on August 31, 1844. His father was an engraver and young George had a talent for art as he frequently drew caricatures and maps in his letters home during the war. He enlisted in Bristol, Rhode Island on August 6, 1862. At the time of his enlistment he stated he was single, eighteen years of age, and a farmer. Spencer was one of many of the Seventh's casualties at Fredericksburg. Unlike many of his comrades however, he was not shot. During the Army of the

[8] Seventh Rhode Island Descriptive Book. Hopkins, *Seventh Rhode Island,* 184-188.
[9] William O. Harrington to Eunice Harrington, June 2, 1864, North Scituate Public Library. George H. Allen, *Forty-Six Months with the Fourth Rhode Island Volunteers in the War of 1861 to 1865.* (Providence: J.A. & R.A. Reid, 1887), 309-310.

Potomac's hasty evacuation from the city on December 15, 1862, scores of Union soldiers separated from their commands were captured by the Confederates. Spencer was one of three Seventh soldiers captured during the battle.[10]

Young Spencer only remained a prisoner of war for several weeks when he was released on parole and ordered to Annapolis, Maryland to await his exchange. He returned to duty in the spring of 1863, but as the Seventh was then on duty in Kentucky, Spencer and several other Seventh soldiers performed garrison duty in the defenses of Washington, and he was present in the city during the Gettysburg Campaign. He joined the Seventh Rhode Island in Kentucky in the fall of 1863, performing garrison duty at Point Burnside, and was present throughout the Overland Campaign of 1864.[11]

The two letters presented below are transcribed from the originals in the author's collection. They were both written in the trenches at Cold Harbor the day before and the day after the horrific June 3, 1864 battle and show the effect of the Overland Campaign on one company of the Seventh Rhode Island Volunteers. Notes have been added to identify the people mentioned in the letters. All cemetery information recorded in the notes has been researched using findagrave.com. All of the men mentioned below served in Company I of the Seventh Rhode Island unless otherwise noted.

Letter I.

Camp of the 7th Regt. R.I.in Rifle Pits near the

Chickahominy June 2d 1864

---

[10] George A. Spencer, Letters in author's collection. George A. Spencer, Service File, National Archives and Records Administration, Washington, DC.
[11] Spencer Letters and Spencer Service File.

Dear Parents

   I am well and these few lines will find you the same. We fell back from our first line of Rifle Pits this morning early because the Rebs were getting too many for us. They drove in our pickets last night but we caught one of them before he could get back his lines again. They followed us up and are now in the pits that we was yesterday. One our pickets have just come in wounded in the cheek.[12] James Gladding[13] is well and so is James Hoard.[14]

   The news has just come that Lee has got 50.000 more men reinforcement.[15] If that is so you not surprised at seeing us taking

---

[12] Private William Welden of Providence was a single, nineteen-year-old laborer who enlisted as a recruit on September 7, 1863. He was shot in the face at Cold Harbor and was also wounded in the arm on October 1, 1864 at Poplar Spring Church. He was mustered out on July 13, 1865. Seventh Rhode Island Descriptive Book.

[13] When he enlisted on August 16, 1862, James H. Gladding of Bristol stated he was an eighteen-year-old single laborer. He was wounded at Fredericksburg on December 13, 1862 and was slightly wounded at Spotsylvania Court House on May 12, 1864. Gladding was mortally wounded in action at Bethesda Church and died of his wounds at Mount Pleasant Hospital in Washington, DC on July 3, 1864. He is interred at North Burial Ground in Bristol, RI. Seventh Rhode Island Descriptive Book.

[14] Private James Hoard Jr. of Bristol volunteered on August 16, 1862. He stated he was single, nineteen years of age, and a "hostler" by occupation. His right arm was amputated at Bethesda Church and he was discharged for disability on April 3, 1865. Hoard returned to Bristol and became a police officer, spending many years as chief of police, and was also very active as a member of Major Jacob Babbitt Post # 15 of the Grand Army of the Republic. He died July 29, 1907 and is interred at North Burial Ground in Bristol. Seventh Rhode Island Descriptive Book. *Providence Journal,* July 31, 1907.

[15] General Robert E. Lee of Virginia commanded the Army of Northern Virginia during the Overland Campaign of 1864. Despite taking enormous casualties, the Army of the Northern Virginia received regular reinforcements during the campaign taken from other parts of the Confederacy. Alfred C. Young III, *Lee's Army During the Overland Campaign: A Numerical Study.* (Baton Rouge: Louisiana State University Press, 2013), 1-26.

the back track. We find Old Lee fortified every where we go. I guess our Batterys killed more of our own men yesterday than they did of the Rebels. Three was killed in the next Regt to us by one of our own shells. The batterys are planted about a half a mile in the rear of us and throw the shell over us, and they don't fix the fuse right, and they burst before they get to the Rebel lines. Them shirts will come all right I guess. Have you sent that map yet. I wrote A letter yesterday to you so you will get two pretty close together. I don't know of any thing else to say at present. So good bye. Give my love to all enquiring friends and take a share for yourselves. Write soon as you get this.

From your son

G.A. Spencer

Co. I 7th Regt. R.I. Vols.
9th Corps

Washington
D.C

P.S. have you got that $5.00 Confederate money I sent you.
G.A. Spencer

Co. I 7th R.I. Vol.
1st Brigade
2nd Division   Washington
9th Corps   D.C.

P.S.S. I see by the papers that we must have been under fire because they had seen some names of wounded. I guess if the man that wrote that piece had been where we have been for the past 2 weeks, he think we have been under fire. They have just brought one more of our Regt dead. Corporal Reynolds shot through the head.[16]

---

[16] Corporal Edward S. Reynolds of Scituate was a single, eighteen-year-old carder who worked in a mill in Scituate when he enlisted on August 14, 1862. He was killed in action while on picket duty near Cold Harbor,

G.A. Spencer

Letter II.

> Camp of the 7th Rhode Island Volunteers
> On the Battle Field
>
> June 4th 1864

Dear Parents

I am well and hope these few lines will find you the same. We was in the fight all day yesterday and would be to day if the Rebels had not Skedaddled.

I am very sorry to say that Co. I has not been so lucky this time as heretofore. We have lost 10 wounded and some very bad. Jimmy Gladding had his arm broken. I did not see him when it was done. I had just left him and he was carried off to the hospital. James Hoard was wounded in the arm bad. The following are the rest of the wounded in Co. I

Alexander Manchester. Bad. Arm and Hip.[17]
H. Winnsemann. Hips.[18]
Ezra Sherman Arm.[19]

Virginia on June 2, 1864 and is buried in an unknown grave at Cold Harbor National Cemetery. Seventh Rhode Island Descriptive Book.

[17] Alexander Manchester resided in Bristol, RI and enlisted on August 18, 1862. He stated that he was a laborer, nineteen years of age, and was single. Manchester was sent to Washington, DC where he died of his wounds on June 15, 1864. His remains were returned to Bristol and interred in North Burial Ground. Seventh Rhode Island Descriptive Book.

[18] A twenty-three-year-old married laborer from Bristol when he enlisted on August 16, 1862, Private Henry Winnsemann had been wounded at Fredericksburg on December 13, 1862. After his wound at Bethesda Church, Winnsemann was shot again, this time through both thighs at Petersburg on June 16, 1864. He was mustered out of the service on June 9, 1865. Seventh Rhode Island Descriptive Book.

E.C. Knight. Hand.[20]
W.H. Northrup. Hand.[21]
R. Hanning Bad Bruise in Side.[22]
Sergeant McIlroy leg.[23]

---

[19] Private Ezra H. Sherman of Bristol was nineteen when he enlisted on August 19, 1862. He was single and a farmer by trade. Sherman was wounded at Fredericksburg in December 1862 and shot in the chest at Petersburg on June 17, 1864. He survived and was mustered out on June 9, 1865. He died June 21, 1909 and is buried at North Burial Ground in Bristol. Seventh Rhode Island Descriptive Book.

[20] Elisha C. Knight was twenty-six, married, and a laborer in Coventry when he volunteered on August 13, 1862. He was wounded twice at Petersburg, on June 16 and June 22, 1864. He was mustered out on June 9, 1865 and returned to Coventry. Knight eventually lived in the house now known as the Paine House of the Western Rhode Island Civic Historical Society. He died on May 29, 1917 and is interred at Pine Grove Cemetery in Coventry, RI. Seventh Rhode Island Descriptive Book. *Providence Journal,* May 30, 1917.

[21] William H. Northrup enlisted as a private on August 16, 1862. He was twenty-three, married, and a laborer at the time. Shot in the hand at Bethesda Church, he was sent to a hospital in Washington where he remained until mustered out on May 14, 1865. He died July 18, 1903 and is interred at Elm Grove Cemetery in North Kingstown, RI. Seventh Rhode Island Descriptive Book.

[22] Corporal Robert Hanning of Newport enlisted August 12, 1862. He was twenty-six, single, and a "coachman." He served in the Seventh's Color Guard and was mustered out on June 9, 1865. Seventh Rhode Island Descriptive Book.

[23] Samuel McIlroy of Pawtucket was one of the first men to enlist in the Seventh Rhode Island on June 10, 1862. At the time, he was married and worked as an engraver. A native of Ireland, McIlroy had served in the British Army and won steady promotion in the Seventh Rhode Island. He was wounded in the head at Fredericksburg. He won a battlefield promotion on May 12, 1864 at Spotsylvania to second lieutenant. His Bethesda Church wound never healed properly, but McIlroy stayed with the Seventh Rhode Island throughout the summer of 1864. Promoted to first lieutenant of Company I in July 1864, he commanded the company until he was mortally wounded at Poplar Spring Church. McIlroy died at City Point, Virginia on October 25, 1864 and his remains were returned to Pawtucket and buried at Mineral Spring Cemetery. He left behind a widow and five children. Hopkins, *Seventh Rhode Island,* 368. Edwin W.

Sergeant James Phelps- finger.[24]
We had none killed

We lost over 50 out of the Regt.

I received your letters and the short and pocket handkerchief and a letter from Miss Julia Gladding also yesterday afternoon about half an hour after Jimmy was wounded. Tell Mrs. Gladding I will see Jimmy if I can get a chance. I have just seen one of the hospital men and he says that Jimmy will have to have his army taken off above Elbo (his right arm) I am very sorry for him. It is a wonder we all did not get killed.

I took one of Jimmy's shirts as they will have to be left here. I thought I had better have it that to throw it away. If I see him I will give it to him and I also took his thread book.
James Hoard took all his things with him when he went off the field. Peleg Jones[25] wants you to tell his wife he is all right and send his love to her. Seymour[26] and James Card[27] wanted me

---

Stone, *Rhode Island in the Rebellion.* (Providence: George. H. Whitney, 1865), 408-409.
[24] Sergeant James T. Phelps resided in Bristol and enlisted on August 15, 1862. At the time he was single, twenty-one, and a jeweler. After Bethesda Church, he was shot in the hand at Petersburg on June 16, 1864 and promoted to lieutenant. He commanded Company I after the mortal wounding of Lieutenant McIlroy and was mustered out on June 9, 1864. He died in 1916 and is interred at North Burial Ground in Bristol. Seventh Rhode Island Descriptive Book.
[25] Corporal Peleg G. Jones was a married carpenter from Bristol and thirty-one when he enlisted on August 15, 1862. He survived the war unscathed and was mustered out on June 9, 1865. He died in 1902 and is interred at North Burial Ground in Bristol, RI. Seventh Rhode Island Descriptive Book. For more information on Jones, refer to Claire Gilbert Dietz, "The Civil War Letters of Peleg G. Jones, Jr." *Rhode Island Roots,* Vol. 34, No. 2 (June 2008), 76-90.
[26] Private Joseph R. Seymour of Bristol was a twenty-four-year-old married farmer who enlisted on August 19, 1862. He was mustered out on June 9, 1865. Seymour died in 1918 and is interred at South Burial Ground in Warren, RI. Seventh Rhode Island Descriptive Book.

to mention their names and say they are all right. I was very glad to get that shirt I tell you. I did not expect it so soon. I very much obliged to you for sending it when you did.

When you write send me some envelopes as don't get much sugar now. I would like to have you send me a head of Navy tobacko so I can trade it for sugar. As the boys some of them would rather have a chew of tobacko than to have there breakfast. Just leave the ends so they can see what it is and it wont cost much that is the only way I know of getting sugar and I cant drink coffee without it. I don't know of any thing more to write at present so good bye. Give my love to all enquiring friends and take a share for yourselves. Write soon

From your Son

G.A. Spencer

Co. I 7 Regt. R.I. Vols.
1st Brigade 2d Division 9th Corps

Washington

PS- Tell Mrs. Gladding I will see Jimmy and give the letter to him and tell Mrs. Hoard I will see James to and all the rest if I possibly can. G.A. Spencer.

George A. Spencer was a survivor. Unlike many members of the regiment, he survived the campaign unscathed, while his good friend James Gladding was mortally wounded at Bethesda Church, and his other close comrade James Hoard had his arm amputated. It was a terrible day for the young man and a bloody day for Company I. The horrors of war would continue to afflict

---

[27] James T. Card enlisted as a private in Company I on August 19, 1862. At the time he resided in Bristol, was single, twenty-two years old, and a cooper. He was mustered out on June 9, 1865 and died in 1918. Like many of his comrades in Company I, Card was interred in North Burial Ground in Bristol. Seventh Rhode Island Descriptive Book.

the men from Bristol and Newport. After the assault at Bethesda Church, the Seventh remained at Cold Harbor, where more men were lost, including Private Allen Pierce, another comrade from Bristol who was killed on June 6, 1864. After a terrifying week in the trenches at Cold Harbor, the Seventh turned south once again to Petersburg, where they settled in for the long siege, losing men almost daily. At Poplar Spring Church on September 30, 1864, the Seventh helped plug a critical gap in the Union line, while Company I's commander, First Lieutenant Samuel McIlroy, whose Bethesda Church never healed was shot again in the leg; this time the wound was mortal. Lieutenant McIroy, an Irish immigrant who resided in Pawtucket, died on November 25, 1864, leaving a wife and five children. Private Spencer survived to be mustered out with the regiment on June 9, 1865.[28]

After the war, George Spencer returned to Bristol, and then relocated to Attleboro, Massachusetts where he found work in the jewelry trade. Unlike many members of the Seventh Rhode Island, Spencer was not active in the Seventh Rhode Island Veterans Association and never attended a regimental reunion. He died of "kidney disease" on September 19, 1914 and was interred in North Burial Ground in Bristol near many veterans of Company I, Seventh Rhode Island Volunteers. His letters, preserved for the last 150 years tell of the horrifying events that happened to the Seventh Rhode Island during the bloody struggle to take Richmond in the spring and summer of 1864.[29]

[28] Company I, Seventh Rhode Island Volunteers, Descriptive Book, Rhode Island State Archives. Hopkins, *Seventh Rhode Island,* 192-223.
[29] Roster of Survivors, Seventh Rhode Island Veterans Association, 1896, author's collection. Death Certificate of George A. Spencer, September 19, 1914, Bristol Town Hall, Bristol, RI.

Chapter Twelve:

"Here we lost many good men:"

A new account from the Battle of Fredericksburg

Ever since my book, *The Seventh Rhode Island Infantry in the Civil War* was published by McFarland in 2008, it opened a literal floodgate of material relating to the Seventh Rhode Island. In that time my private collection has grown tremendously and I have crisscrossed the country gathering almost every scrap of paper I could find regarding the regiment. Even better, advances in technology have brought to light many new contemporary newspaper accounts on the Seventh Rhode Island. The result of all of this research has produced several file cabinets full of new and useful material that will one day be used to write an updated unit history.

Among the many resources not available to me when I wrote my book in 2006-2007 were the absolutely fantastic and vital papers of Major Thomas Fry Tobey contained within the Beinecke Rare Book and Manuscript Library at Yale University in New Haven, Connecticut. Covering nearly his entire life, the Tobey papers provide a great deal of material relevant to Seventh Rhode Island. Among the gems found within was a long letter that Tobey penned to his brother John a week after the Battle of Fredericksburg. Transcribed and edited below, this letter contains the best descriptions I have ever found regarding the Seventh Rhode Island at Fredericksburg.[1]

---

[1] "Introduction to the Thomas Fry Tobey Papers," http://drs.library.yale.edu/fedora/get/beinecke:tobey/PDF, accessed January 27, 2017.

Thomas Fry Tobey was the son of Dr. Samuel Boyd Tobey and Sarah Earl Fry Tobey. He was born in Providence on September 30, 1840. The Tobey family was "eminent Quakers," and Thomas took part in the faith growing up. He attended Brown University and graduated from there in 1859; among his acquaintances was John Hay whom would later serve as private secretary to Abraham Lincoln, as well as United States Secretary of State. He graduated from Harvard Law School in 1861 and went into the practice of law with his brother John F. Tobey.[2]

On May 26, 1862, Tobey volunteered, against his parent's wishes, to serve three months as a member of the Tenth Rhode Island Volunteers; he served as a sergeant in Company D. Hastily raised within forty-eight hours and rushed to Washington. Tobey's brother John served as adjutant of the regiment. The Tenth, as well as its sister regiment the Ninth spent their term of service garrisoning the city before being mustered out on August 30, 1862. Tobey remained with the Tenth when he reported back to Rhode Island. Here he assisted in raising a company for the Seventh Rhode Island. Tobey became a captain in the Seventh and was placed in command of Company E, a group of men raised in the Blackstone Valley towns of Cumberland, Woonsocket, and Smithfield. He defended his decision to his parents to take a commission in the Seventh, "I hope you will both do me the justice to believe that I have not chosen lightly in this important matter, and that it is not a boyish impulse, but a sense of duty to my country, that sends me into certain discomfort and danger, and possible death."[3]

Tobey received his commission on September 4, and left Rhode Island with the regiment a week later. The officers of the

---

[2] William P. Hopkins, *The Seventh Regiment Rhode Island Volunteers in the Civil War: 1862-1865.* (Providence: Snow & Farnum, 1903), 326-327. Thomas F. Tobey to John Hay, April 8, 1862 and June 28, 1864, Hay Library, Brown University, Providence, RI.

[3] Descriptive Book of Company E, Seventh Rhode Island Volunteers, Rhode Island State Archives, Providence, RI. Thomas F. Tobey to Parents, July 11, 1862, Beinecke Rare Book and Manuscript Library, Yale University, New Haven, CT.

Seventh had drawn lots to determine their seniority, with Tobey and Company E becoming the sixth ranked captain, as well as the sixth company in line. After performing garrison duty around Washington and joining the Army of the Potomac's Ninth Corps in October 1862, the Seventh set out for Fredericksburg, arriving opposite the city in late November.[4]

In volunteering for service in the Seventh Rhode Island, Tobey was literally excommunicated. At a meeting of the Society of Friends (Quakers) in Providence, a committee put before the entire membership that "his present position is incompatible with membership in our religious society." Because he had broken the Quaker vows to remain peaceful and not take up arms, the Society voted to "disown thee as a member of our religious society." Tobey would find religion again late in life.[5]

At 12:20 on the afternoon of December 13, 1862, the Seventh Rhode Island was ordered to the front as part of the assault at Marye's Heights. Of 570 officers and men who took part in the battle, forty-nine were killed or mortally wounded, 145 were wounded, and three were captured. Tobey's Company E lost five dead and seventeen wounded.[6]

A week after the battle, Tobey wrote back to his brother John in Providence and told him about his experiences in the battle. This letter provides the most vivid, detailed account of the Seventh's role at Fredericksburg. Unlike most Union soldiers, Tobey does not shirk in describing his fear and feelings that he felt during the battle, as well as the horrors he witnessed that day. It paints a moving, touching image of the terrible carnage faced by the Seventh Rhode Island at Fredericksburg. This letter has been

---

[4] Hopkins, *Seventh Rhode Island,* 1-22. Zenas R. Bliss, *The Reminiscences of Major General Zenas R. Bliss, 1854-1876.* Edited by Thomas T. Smith, Jerry Thompson, Robert Wooster, and Ben E. Pingenot. (Austin: Texas State Historical Association, 2007), 312-315.
[5] Samuel Austin to Thomas F. Tobey, December 20, 1862, Beinecke Rare Book and Manuscript Library, Yale University.
[6] Hopkins, *Seventh Rhode Island,* 57-59. Company E Seventh Rhode Island Descriptive Book. *Providence Journal,* December 19-30, 1862.

transcribed from the original at the Beinecke Rare Book and Manuscript Library with footnotes added to identify the men Tobey described.

Camp near Fredericksburg Va., Dec. 20th 1862

My Dear John,

I have been too busy since the action to find time for more than a few hurried notes. To day, however, there seems a little more chance to write, and I will improve it by trying to give you some slight account of my share in the events of the last weeks.

To begin at the beginning. Last Wedesday night of last week we were ordered to have 3 days cooked ration ready and served out, with 60 rounds of ammunition. Thursday morning about 2 o'clock, I was awakened by the sound of the guns. Such a cannonade I never found any conception of. The rapidity of the discharges was more like musketry than like artillery fire. (This firing continued till evening with scarcely any cesation). Towards 8 o'clock we were formed into line and sent out to front- as that was next morning and advanced up on the hill just out of range of the rebel guns where we remained all day, expecting every moment to be ordered to charge across the bridge as some as it should be them across. At night we were ordered back to quarters. Leaving, as you hear, the bridge across and over troops in the town. (By the way, while we were waiting that day, I saw the first sight I ever saw in the military line- a brigade of cavalry advancing in line. It was a noble site + their horses kept their alignment better than any infantry of the same length of front that I have ever seen)

Before daylight next morning (Friday- we formed in line again- had whiskey served out to the men- and marched over the hill and down through a ravine to the pontoon bridge. The firing had ceased, except an occasional gun. Just as we got across the bridge, the rebs sent half a dozen shells from the batteries beyond the town, which passed over our heads, all but one or tell which

160

fell in the water close to us. They had a beautifully accurate range. However we got safely across.

Well, I have partially fixed my assets. But I would give an order on the Paymaster for $20.00 (or twenty five cents in cash) for an hour's talk with you. I could tell you a great many things that I don't dare write, which might open your eyes, as mine have been opened. I dare say you think I am mistaken, but oblige me by keeping this letter till the war is over (a day I don't expect to see, but which I hope you will). The mouths of the army will be unsealed then. But we must pass through great suffering first. Woe to the nations that is cursed with corruption in high places.

Well enough of this. To return to Fredericksburg. In the afternoon as we were sitting, smoking, and waiting the troops coming over the hill cross over us. One brigade band marched over in great style, playing Yankee Doodle. It sounded fine, and so did the rebel shell that came over our heads in about two minutes and struck right into the column, skedaddaling the band, and killing one of the soldiers. I never head music quit so quick.[7] Then for a few minutes the shells did come over us lively, hitting none on our side the river however. In a little while our heavy batteries on the other side silence the rebel batteries, and we had no more trouble that day. Towards evening we marched down in to the centre of the town and quartered ourselves for the night.

Saturday morning, after a short season of pillaging, our brigade was found and marched towards the outskirts of the town (still near the river bank) where we halted and waited for orders. Here Gen. Meagher's brigade came along and halted beside us, and the General made them a short speech.[8] It was a very

---

[7] This was the band of the Twelfth New Hampshire Volunteers. Hopkins, *Seventh Rhode Island*, 40.

[8] Brigadier General Thomas Francis Meagher, 1823-1867, was the leader of the Irish Brigade, composed of the 63rd, 69th, and 88th New York, as well as the 28th Massachusetts, and the 116th Pennsylvania. He was an Irish revolutionary, who fled to America, becoming a leader in the New York Irish community. See Timothy Eagan, *The Immortal Irishman: The*

interesting speech, and the more interesting to us from the fact that our division was to follow theirs. Meagher is a fine looking fellow, and a great dandy- dresses entirely in black, with a silver star on each shoulder (no shoulder straps) and looks altogether like a black Brunswicker. By the way, the artillery and musketry began to sound heavy towards the front, and the shot and shell were constantly flying over us. Off went the Irish Brigade and very soon the firing grew still heavier, and the shot and shell began to drop even into our sheltered position. Lieut. Kenyon[9] was wounded here and one private killed + two or three wounded.[10] It was pretty tiresome to sit doing nothing + have the men hit. But before long up came the order to move.

So we fell into line, face by the right flank, and started up a side street towards the front (Each regiment of our brigade moved up a separate street). The shell whistled smartly over our heads, but no one was struck at first. Thank God the distance was not long, for the shot enfiladed at first. We had gone a little way, when a shell burst a few yards in front of me, covering me and my 1st sergeant with mud,[11] and filling my eyes with mud and gravel. A few fragments of stone or a piece of the shell (I don't know which, but I fancy the former) also scratched my left hand. When the dirt flew in my eyes, I instinctively raised my hand to my face, and staggered, but someone called out "the Captain's hit," and that

---

Irish Revolutionary Who Became an American Hero. (New York: Houghton, Mifflin, Harcourt, 2016).

[9] David R. Kenyon, 1833-1897, was originally the first lieutenant of Company A. A native of Richmond, RI he was a mill superintendent before the war. Wounded at Fredericksburg, he was promoted to captain of Company I, but resigned on March 2, 1863. Hopkins, *Seventh Rhode Island,*

[10] The first man killed in the Seventh Rhode Island was Private Nicholas W. Matthewson, a farmer was West Greenwich who served in Company F. The same shell wounded Nicholas' brother Calvin, as well as James W. Bates, also of Company F. Hopkins, *Seventh Rhode Island,* 43.

[11] The first sergeant of Company E was Charles L. Porter, a twenty-one-year-old shoemaker from Burrillville. Porter was wounded at Bethesda Church on June 3, 1864 and survived to be mustered out on June 9, 1865. He later moved to Thompson, Connecticut and died there in 1900. Company E Descriptive Book.

set me on my legs again. I said, "No, I'm not hurt," and started ahead, rubbing my eyes.

In two or three second (for these things which I see happened in almost no time), and just as I was showing my hand to Lieut. Wilbur,[12] and saying "First blood for Co. E Wilby," a big rifled projectile came walking down the street, taking steps of 20 yards or thereabouts. For a thing that came too fast to be dodged, it did not take a while to get past from the moment it first have in sight. I could think of nothing but a shark. It first struck a fence in the left near Col. Bliss,[13] went by him and over the regiment to the other side of the street, struck a building on that side, turned and next past the left of my company within about a foot of Lieut. Daniels,[14] passing between him and my 3d sergeant, and hurt no one in our Regiment after all.

---

[12] George A. Wilbur, 1830-1906, of Woonsocket was the second lieutenant of Company E. Wilbur had a harrowing Civil War career. He was shot in the thigh at Fredericksburg, and nearly died of disease contracted in Mississippi in 1863. He ended the war as captain of Company K. A lawyer before the war, he later became an associate justice of the Rhode Island Supreme Court and was highly active in veteran's affairs. Hopkins, *Seventh Rhode Island,* 357-358.

[13] Colonel Zenas Randall Bliss, 1835-1900, of Johnston was the commander of the Seventh Rhode Island. An 1854 West Point graduate he had served on the Texas frontier before returning to Rhode Island in 1862 to command the Tenth and later the Seventh Rhode Island Regiments. A born leader, Bliss was universally beloved by his men. He earned the Medal of Honor leading the regiment at Fredericksburg. Mustered out of volunteer service in 1865, he spent much of the next three decades in Texas commanding the Buffalo Soldiers. Bliss is buried at Arlington National Cemetery. Hopkins, *Seventh Rhode Island,* 311-314.

[14] Percy Daniels, 1840-1916, served as the first lieutenant of Company E during the battle. A native of Woonsocket, he was an engineer before the war. Daniels was promoted to captain after the battle and later to lieutenant colonel. He commanded the regiment from May 1864 through the rest of the war, but was not respected by the men. He later moved to Kansas and became involved in politics. Hopkins, *Seventh Rhode Island,* 322-325. Stephen Farnum Peckham, "Recollections of a Hospital Steward in the Civil War," Newport Historical Society, Newport, RI.

Well we couldn't stop to look after it, we were too near the enemy so in a moment more we filed to the right and crossed a railway cut (where our men began to fall), on to the field where we lay down behind a little ridge, having got there before the rest of the brigade. Indeed Ferrero[15] whom we were to follow, brought his brigade past us while we were laying there. You should have seen him take them in. He is brave, if ever a man was. So instead of having to follow the 2d Maryland (which didn't get on the field at all) + the 6th NH + 48th Pennsylvania, as the Herald correspondent says, our regiment was under fire more than half an hour before one of them came up.

Well, we lay there, waiting to be ordered up to help Ferrero and now I had plenty of time to think. Now I am going to tell you how I felt and what I did for I know you will want to know, and as I believe I did my duty I shall say so. You will know what I mean, but don't say anything about it to anyone not of the family, for a stranger would think it foolish and vain talk, but you know I don't mean it for that.

I think the first thing that surprised me was that there was not more noise. To be sure there was a heavy fire of artillery and musketry over the ridge in front and solid shot, grape, rifle balls, + all sorts of projectiles were flying over us, and shrapnel and case shot bursting about our heads, but my notions were formed from Thursday's cannonade, and I had expected a defining roar. (I heard noise enough later in the day) My next surprise was that I didn't feel afraid. I was anxious, especially for my men of whom some had fallen so far, and rather expected to be hit every moment, but I felt no fear. Before we were ordered up, while waiting in the street, Kenyon was hit. I felt very nervous and uneasy, and had feared the feeling would grow on me when I got to the field.

Coming up the street I had been too busy keeping my files closed to think of anything else, except once, when the thought

---

[15] Brigadier General Edward Ferrero, 1831-1899, commanded the Second Brigade, Second Division, Ninth Corps at the Battle of Fredericksburg. He was relieved of command in 1864 for his failure at the Battle of the Crater. *New York Times,* December 13, 1899.

flashed through my mind whether the first man I saw shot would sicken me (which it didn't), but now that I had nothing to do but to keep my men still, I was I confess agreeably surprised to find that if not indifferent to the danger, I at least did not fear it excessively.

Here Wilbur was hit. I was lying a few feet front of the company, he was in his place as a file closer, lying nearly behind me. A shrapnel shell, or a case shot, I don't know enough about artillery to tell which, burst over our heads and threw bullets +c all round us. I turned round + asked if any one was hurt- no one answered and I was about to say something when Wilbur cut me short by saying, "My God Captain, I'm wounded." I detailed 4 men and had him carried off the field. I confess, as I saw him carried off, I thought, 'well I suppose my time will come next,' but I cheered myself up with the thought that I was doing my duty.

It was in this field that Lieut. Col. Sayles was killed.[16] Thank God I did not see him fall. Col. Bliss had a very narrow escape from being killed by the same shell. He was talking to the Lieut. Col. only a few moments before. They had a battery on our right that enfiladed us, and our loss would have been terrible had we lain there much longer.

Well after about half an hour or more of time, as I said, I heard the Colonel's voice, as cool as if at battalion drill call out, "Battalion." Up jumped every man in a moment, not a man flinched. "Forward, guide centre, march," and off we went to the front, guiding on an old calico rag, that we have carried for 3

---

[16] Lieutenant Colonel Welcome Ballou Sayles, 1812-1862, was the second in command of the Seventh Rhode Island. A prominent member of the Providence Democratic Party, Ballou had been an active participant in the Dorr Rebellion, and published the *Providence Press* before joining the Seventh Rhode Island. At Fredericksburg he was hit in the chest by a Parrott shell fired from Marye's Heights and was eviscerated, pieces of his body flying over members of the regiment, including Colonel Bliss who was covered head to toe in Sayles viscera. Hopkins, *Seventh Rhode Island,* 314-315.

months.[17] Over a fence into the next field and then came the order, "by the right flank march." The men were dropping pretty fast, but the regiment faced by the flank + marched off with perfect steadiness. Talk about it being impossible to drill under fire, but our regiment did it at Fredericksburg.

We moved by the flank until we got, I should think, nearly opposite to the battery that had worried us, and then marched by the left flank straight up towards the enemy (all this was done at the double quick, and better executed that I ever saw the regiment execute any maneuver of equal difficulty at battalion drill). Right in front of us was a rail fence, about 3 rails high, over which we had to climb, and here we lost many good men (I believe Manchester was hit here),[18] but we got well over this and formed line on the other side.

When we got on the other side however, I found that my company, being on the extreme left was separated by a board fence from the rest of the regiment. Supposing however that the regiment would advance straight forward, I started off with my company, along the line of this fence (at right angles to the one we had just climbed + on in line of battle), through an orchard, past a swail, and up to the crest of the hill in front of the batteries. Here I

---

[17] The Seventh Rhode Island had not been given a flag when they left Rhode Island in September 1862. To make up for this, the members of Company D, the Color Company of the regiment, purchased a small American flag in Baltimore when the regiment passed through the city. It was nailed to rake handle and carried into battle at Fredericksburg by Sergeant Frederic Weigand. It was nearly ripped in half by a shell and hit by sixteen bullets. Weigand received a battlefield commission for his heroism at Fredericksburg. The flag was known as the "Fredericksburg Flag." A larger, proper National color was received in January 1863 from the "Ladies of Providence." Today both flags are at the Rhode Island State House. Displayed under less than ideal conditions, they are quite literally rotting to pieces. Hopkins, *Seventh Rhode Island,* 291-293.
[18] Sergeant Major Joseph Swift Manchester, 1841-1872, of Bristol lost his left arm at Fredericksburg. He later became a captain in the commissary department. Hopkins, *Seventh Rhode Island,* 363.

found 3 companies of the 12th (the only companies from that regiment that were in the action) who had just got up.[19]

I halted, called to my men to hurry up + being lighter than the average I had them dressed than, and gave the order "commence firing." There for the first time I felt I and my company could go through any fire or do anything that men can do and more to. I felt big, no phrase will express it. I stood there and wave my sword and talked to my men as uncowardly as if I were a thousand miles from danger.

In the meanwhile I tried to see if I could see our Regiment beyond the fence to our right. Not being able to, I called for a man who would go to death with a message for Col. Bliss. Half a dozen of my men sprang forward in a moment. I picked out a smart active boy and told him to get to the other side of the fence and find where the Regiment was, and then to report to me. "I'll do it Captain, and come back if I live," said he, and off he went. In a few minutes he came back safe (and came out of the fight safe, I am glad to say) and repeated that after we crossed the fence, the regiment had aligned to the right and was now on the same alignment with us, but some little distance to the right.

So I called my company into line, faced them by the right flank, and off we started. Into the next field, and there were the colors on the ridge. "Company by the left flank march- now follow me boys," said I, as loud as I could yell, and we charged up through the field. I tell you that was rough. As I started to lead the Company up, I could hear the rifle balls and the grape whistling by my head, and could see them cutting up the dirt on all sides, and at my very feet. I fancied I felt the wind of one ball at my cheek. The

---

[19] Although the Twelfth Rhode Island lost twenty men killed and over eighty wounded at Fredericksburg, the regiment disintegrated under fire, men fled for their lives under fire. A nine-month regiment, the Twelfth was led by Colonel George Browne, a former Congressman. Poorly equipped, and poorly led, the Twelfth's flight was recorded by many Rhode Island soldiers. Pardon E. Tillinghast, *History of the Twelfth Regiment Rhode Island Volunteers in the Civil War 1862-1863.* (Providence: Snow & Farnum, 1904), 37-45.

thought came into my mind, 'This is death. A man might as well hope to go through a hailstorm untouched as to get to that ridge unhurt.' But I knew my place was ahead of my men, and I kept there, though it cost me an effort, for a moment. I was badly scared but I kept on waving my sword, and calling to my men to keep up and though they fell all around me, I reached the ridge safely.

As soon as I got on the ridge, to the left of Co. A, I looked round, my company was close behind me, coming up in good shape, but now reduced. I noticed in an instant that a number of the men were done. In coming up I had only seen one fall (and <u>felt</u> another, who fell against me as he went down) but now I could recognize the figures of some of my men and I knew more must be down that I didn't know of. But I had no time to feel heart sick-that came next day. I held up my sword for to mark the rallying point for the company (the only use I know of for an officer's sword), got them together, and ordered them to lie down. Then after resting there for a moment I have them to order to commence firing again. We were I should think in very much such a position as Burnside's brigade at Bull Run.[20] We lay under the crest of a little ridge where we could rise up to fire, and lie down to load. The ridge was not protection enough to keep men from being hit while lying down, but it was better than none. In every place it dipped men were there. The 12th Regt was quite well sheltered.

Before us was a valley, at the bottom of which was a canal, lay the rebel infantry line, and back of them, on the top of a steep hill, were their batteries. The position was too strong for us. As the Colonel says, "They might have defended such a position by rolling stones down in us."

---

[20]At Bull Run, on July 21, 1861, Ambrose Burnside had led a brigade consisting of the Second New Hampshire, Seventy-First New York, as well as the First and Second Rhode Island Regiments. The Second Rhode Island fought alone, for nearly an hour before reinforcements came up. Brent Nosworthy, *Roll Call to Destiny: The Soldier's Eye View of Civil War Battles.* (New York: Basic Books, 2008), 33-83.

Well we lay there and fired away all our ammunition. It sickens me now to think of the waste of the energies and lives. The men behaved splendidly, but what use was it? Every now + then one of my men would turn to me and say "I'm hit Captain," and drop. I heard no cries of pain, nor words of complaint. The men did nobly. I did little the rest of the day, but sit there, talk to the men to encourage them, do what I could for the wounded, and now + then, when I thought the men slackened their fire a little, go forward, and call on them to come up and fire. In fact that was all there was to be done. So I had plenty of time to look about. I was surprised (in fact the battle spent a great many of my previous ideas) to see how little confusion there was, and how easily I noticed everything going on anywhere near me.

The first man I saw was the Colonel. I don't know what to say about him. I can't say anything half good enough. He came out large that day. He took the regiment in nobly and showed courage which I don't believe can well be beaten. The second bravest men I saw that day were Col. Barnes[21] (commanding a brigade in Griffin's division, I believe)[22] who rode by us several times at a slow trot- he was the only mounted officer I saw. Col. Potter of the 51st NY[23] and a sergeant of the 51st. But I saw very few men who were not brave. How could our regiment at any rate fail to do its duty with such a Colonel to set an example? Major Babbitt, too behaved finely.[24] The Colonel told me he was satisfied with my

---

[21] Colonel James Barnes, 1801-1869, led the 18th Massachusetts Regiment during the Civil War. A West Pointer, he later became a brigadier general and was wounded at Gettysburg. Ezra J. Warner, *Generals in Blue: Lives of the Union Commanders.* (Baton Rouge: Louisiana State University Press, 1964), 20-21

[22] Charles Griffin, 1825-1867, was a West Pointer and career army officer who spent much of the war commanding a division in the Fifth Corps. Warner, *Generals in Blue,* 190-191.

[23] Colonel Robert Brown Potter, 1829-1887, led the Fifty-First New York. He later commanded a brigade and division in the Ninth Corps as a brigadier general. After the war he settled in Newport, Rhode Island where he died. Warner, *Generals in Blue,* 382-383.

[24] Major Jacob Babbitt, 1809-1862, of Bristol had attended Norwich University, graduating in 1826. A wealthy Bristol banker, he was heavily involved in civil affairs in his native town, as well as active in the Rhode

conduct, so I suppose I have the right to say that no officer of our regiment, so far as I know, or have heard, misbehaved that day. But the Colonel was the man that day. Our regiment swears by him ever since that fight.

Soon after we got on the field the 6th NH of our brigade- a splendid regiment- came up in line on our right. It was a fine sight. They marched up in quick time, closing the gaps as men fell, and keeping the alignment unbroken. The 51st NY (Ferrero's old regt) did the same thing when they came up.

Well, I am spinning this out to a tremendous length, and shall never had it done if I go on at this rate. I will close up. During the long hours that we lay there, there was plenty of incidents which I could tell you, but which I will leave until if it please God, I get a chance to tell them to you with my own lips. This letter is entirely egotistical, as I warned you. I make it so because I don't know about what was done outside of Sturgis' Division.[25]

I was cooler and less excited on the field than I had expected. Indeed, I think it must be impossible in battle to realize the full extent of the danger. I have received a good many compliments since the fight for coolness and courage, which I cannot feel that I deserve. I had my duty to do, and tried my best to do it. If I had failed, I should have deserved blame, but I don't feel that I have earned any praise. Two or three times it was not courage, but only a sense of duty that made me express myself.

Island Militia. At Fredericksburg, he was shot in the chest as he attempted to order the 127th Pennsylvania Regiment to stop firing over the heads of the Seventh Rhode Island when they were pinned down in front of Marye's Heights. He died ten days later on December 23, 1862 and was buried in Bristol in one of the largest funeral's Rhode Island has ever seen. Julia Emily Babbitt, *Sketch of Major Jacob Babbitt, 7th Rhode Island Regiment.* (Bristol, RI: NP, 1890), 1-10.

[25] General Samuel D. Sturgis, 1822-1889, commanded the Second Division, Ninth Corps at the Battle of Fredericksburg. He later became colonel of the Seventh Cavalry and his son was killed at the Little Big Horn. Warner, *Generals in Blue,* 486-487.

But you should have seen the Colonel. Three times or more he took a musket, went up on the crest and fired. One of the times a man who was standing next to him was shot down. You can judge how we cheered for him- so conspicuous a mark as he is, too, and close to the colors, which had 16 holes and one shell hole through them. You can judge how ancious we felt for him, the fact that several of us formed and waved our swords to distract the enemy's attention, and I for one, forgot any danger in anxiety for him. "I know it isn't my business," said he, "but I want the men to see I am not afraid." And he is so kind hearted too.

After dark, when our supports had come up, and our cartridges were all gone, and we were still lying in our places, waiting for orders relieving us to come, the enemy's fire slacked a little. I went up to the Colonel who was lying not very far from me, and we had a pleasant talk together. Just in the middle of it- crash!- came a smashing volley from the rebels and their batteries opened again. Talk of hot fire. I never imagined anything like that. Our Regt could do nothing but lie still, but the 51st NY and the other fresh regt which had just relieved us stood up to them splendidly. "Lie down Tom," said the Colonel and down I dropped beside him. We lay there a few minutes, and then the Colonel said, "That battery on our right ought to open on them. Tom, do you think you can get to it?"

I tell you that it was rough. I don't believe any man could have passed alive through that fire down to our right. But of course my duty was clear, so I said) as men do in books, you know) "I don't know Colonel, but I can try." "No," said the Colonel after waiting a moment. "I won't order you to any such service as that." Of course I said that I needed no order to go in any duty that he thought was necessary. "Well, wait a little," said he, and in a moment more, whoo-oo-oo-oo came a shell from one battery over us towards the rebs. "Bully for you," said the Colonel. "That is one of our whistlers. Lie quiet Tom." I can tell you it was a great weight off my chest.

I was just tightening my belt to run that terrible gauntlet, expecting nothing short of certain death, when that shell came. But it was as kind of the Colonel to keep me there till the last moment, as he did. He is bully. It is too bad that he will be lost to us soon- for if there is any decency left in Washington they can't fail to give him his brigade. Well Church[26] will make a good Colonel if Sprague[27] will promote him, but no one can ever replace our Colonel. But we haven't lost him yet.[28]

One more remark, and I have done. Grape is disgusting, shot, shell, canister, shrapnel for me. It sounds more like a flock of quails than anything else I can compare it to, and it makes such nasty sounds. But the sound is what I especially object to. That fluttering noise made me feel uncomfortable than all the other noises of projectiles put together.

Well, I will stop here. I hate to speak of the retreat from the field. Long after dark, when the wounded men had begun to mourn, and almost every step was over the body of a man, and

---

[26] George E. Church, 1835-1910, served as captain of Company C at Fredericksburg. An engineer, he had extensively traveled throughout South America before the Civil War. Given a battlefield commission as lieutenant colonel in the Seventh Rhode Island, Church became colonel of the Eleventh Rhode Island in March 1863, and was mustered out in July 1863. After the war he returned to South America. Today his large collection of South Americana is housed at Brown University. Hopkins, *Seventh Rhode Island,* 315-319.

[27] William Sprague, 1830-1915, served as governor of Rhode Island from 1860-1863, before his election to the United States Senate. As captain-general of the Rhode Island Militia, Sprague had led the First Rhode Island Regiment to war in 1861 and had two horses shot out from under him at Bull Run. As governor of Rhode Island, Sprague approved of and signed the commissions of the officers in the Seventh. Henry Wharton Shoemaker, *The Last of the War Governors: A Biographical Appreciation of Colonel William Sprague.* (Altoona: Altoona Publishing Co., 1916).

[28] Colonel Bliss was nominated for promotion to brigadier general for his gallantry at Fredericksburg, but was turned down for promotion. In addition to earning the Medal of Honor, he also earned a brevet of major in the Regular Army. *Reminiscences,* 333-334.

then came the manly task of visiting the hospitals to find my men where I saw sights that made me wish myself back facing the rebel batteries. Finally, thank God on Monday evening came as safe retreat from that hapless enterprise. There came the reaction. All last week I couldn't hear a sudden noise of any kind without standing. I couldn't hear a gun in the distance without listening for a shell to whiz over my head.

There, I have done. I wanted to give you some little idea of how it felt on the field, because I thought you would like to know. I don't pretend to give you any account of the fight or even of our share in it, but only to tell you of a few little things that might interest you.

Our regiment receives praises from all quarters. The 12th I am sorry to say skeddaddled- all but the 3 right companies. The fault is said to be in their officers. Major Dyer was wounded[29] before reaching the field by a piece of shell which hit him in the leg, but made no bruise or abrasion of the skin, or other external mark. However, he was unable to get to the field. You will be glad to learn that he is well now. Bah! God keep me from ever deserting my post. What a contemptable animal and coward he is!

Well good bye. Love to all at home. I have some bully old letter from the family and my various friends. Write to me when you can. Please send me the Atlantic for December + January- if not too much trouble. Love to Addie- Regards to Parsons + all my friends. Don't show this letter to any one out of the family.

Well, God bless you

Yours

Tom

Merry Christmas

---

[29] Major Cyrus Grinnell Dyer, 1831-1892, was a lawyer in Providence before the war. He had seen prior service in the First and Second Rhode Island Regiments before becoming major of the Twelfth Rhode Island in October 1862. Tillinghast, *Twelfth Rhode Island,* 336.

Immediately after the Battle of Fredericksburg, Colonel Bliss was faced with a crisis in command. The Seventh's two other field officers, Lieutenant Colonel Welcome Ballou Sayles and Major Jacob Babbitt had both died at Fredericksburg. Furthermore, Second Lieutenant Charles H. Kellen was also killed, and eight other officers wounded. In the aftermath of the battle, half of the Seventh's officer corps resigned and went home. Bliss promoted men who had distinguished themselves at Fredericksburg to the lieutenant positions in the Seventh, while moving up several promising lieutenants to captain and company command. As his new lieutenant colonel, Bliss appointed Captain George E. Church. As major, Bliss appointed Thomas F. Tobey who had proved his leadership capabilities at Fredericksburg. In a letter to Governor William Sprague, Bliss wrote of his new major, young and of not much experience, a brave soldier." Tobey quickly purchased the new uniform of his rank and sewed on the gold oak leaves of a major.[30]

In the spring of 1863, Tobey and the Seventh were sent to Kentucky, and in June embarked for Vicksburg. Like dozens of men from the Seventh Rhode Island, Tobey's health was "severely shattered by remittent fever." Major Thomas F. Tobey was discharged for disability contracted in the service on February 9, 1864 at Point Burnside, Kentucky. Tobey returned to Providence, but surprisingly, he enlisted in the United States Army on February 27, 1865. Enlisting as a sergeant in Company F, Second Battalion, Fourteenth Infantry, by May 1865 he was a first lieutenant.

Promotion in the Regulars to higher rank was always excitingly slow, and it was not until 1874 he became a captain. He was active in the Indian Wars of the 1870s and 1880s, seeing combat in Oregon, Arizona, California, Idaho, Montana, and Wyoming. Tobey married Marie Wingard in 1881 and had two children, both of whom died young. He was active in the Masons,

---

[30] Regimental Descriptive Book, Seventh Rhode Island Volunteers, Rhode Island State Archives. Zenas R. Bliss to William Sprague, December 30, 1862, Rhode Island State Archives. Hopkins, *Seventh Rhode Island,* 326-327.

Grand Army of the Republic, as well as the Military Order of the Loyal Legion. Despite his many years of service in the Fourteenth Infantry, Tobey always retained a deep interest in the Seventh Rhode Island. When he found out that the veterans of the regiment had published a history of the Seventh in 1903, Tobey wrote to author William Palmer Hopkins two years later, "I really *must* have the history of the dear old regiment. It was only the other day that I learned that the book had been published. I wonder why I was not notified." After receiving his copy of the book two weeks later, the old soldier wrote back to Hopkins, "I have read it with deepest interest, and how it brought back to me the days of our campaigning together. You have done a most valuable work, which every man of the old Seventh will cherish."

He retired from the United States Army as a captain in 1892, but was placed on the retired list as a major in 1904, allowing Tobey to earn a larger pension. Major Thomas Fry Tobey converted to Catholicism late in life. He died on June 7, 1920 at Sea Isle, New Jersey and is interred at North Burial Ground in Providence, Rhode Island.[31]

---

[31] Hopkins, *Seventh Rhode Island,* 327. *Providence Journal,* June 10, 1920. Thomas F. Tobey to William P. Hopkins, November 1, 1905 and November 20, 1905, author's collection.

Chapter Thirteen:

"With regret I am called to inform you:"

Civil War notification to a Rhode Island family

In the early morning hours of October 19, 1864, a large Confederate force under the command of Jubal Early attacked a Union encampment near Cedar Creek, Virginia. Stunned from the early morning attack, thousands of half-awake, panicked Union soldiers ran for their lives to escape the Rebel onslaught. The day would have been a total route for the Union army if not for the remarkable stand of two Rhode Island batteries and the Old Vermont Brigade. Battery C and Battery G of the First Rhode Island Light Artillery, together with the Vermonters held on long enough for the rest of the Union Army of the Shenandoah to reform on the high ground north of Middletown, Virginia. From that position, the Union forces counterattacked in the afternoon, destroying the remaining Rebel forces in the Shenandoah Valley.[1]

The stand of Battery G at Cedar Creek received praise from all who witnessed it. Colonel Charles H. Tompkins, the regimental commander who was wounded in the battle helping to withdraw Battery G wrote, "The conduct of officers and men was gallant in the extreme and it merits the hearty commendation of all who witnessed it. Rhode Island has just cause to be proud of such soldiers." General Frank Wheaton wrote of Captain George W. Adams, the grizzled tough commander who led the men into the fight, "In my opinion, he has few superiors in the service, and his admirable battery has been so skillfully and gallantly handled in

---

[1] Diary of James A. Barber, October 19, 1864, John Hay Library, Brown University, Providence, RI. Howard Coffin, *Full Duty: Vermonters in the Civil War.* (Woodstock, VT: Countryman Press, 1993), 306-318.

battle. I never saw a battery more ably and desperately fought."
The battery made a heroic stand, but paid with a heavy price: nine
men died, twenty were wounded, and three were captured. Nearly
a third of the men in Battery G went down in the fighting at Cedar
Creek.[2]

     After the battle, Battery C and Battery G were
consolidated into one unit, named Battery G. The command
returned to the siege lines at Petersburg, where on April 2, 1865
Captain Adams led a band of his men on foot as part of a general
assault on the Confederate entrenchments. They managed to
capture two Confederate cannon which were promptly turned on
their former owners. For their part in the attack, seven Rhode
Islanders were awarded the Medal of Honor.[3]

     In 2009, McFarland published my book, *The Boys of
Adams' Battery G: The Civil War through the Eyes of a Union
light artillery unit.* It was the first published account of Battery G,
First Rhode Island Light Artillery in the Civil War, although three
others, including Captain Adams, historian and veteran of both
World Wars General Harold Barker, and television reporter Glenn
Laxton had attempted to write a history, but never did. Because no
prior history of the unit had been published, I based nearly my
entire narrative on primary manuscript sources. The official papers
of the battery from the Rhode Island State Archives proved a
blessing, as did the journals and letters of men such as James
Barber from Brown University, Albert Cordner's papers at the
North Dakota Historical Society, and pension files from the
National Archives.

---

[2] John Russell Bartlett, *Memoirs of Rhode Island Officers Who Were
Engaged in the Service of Their Country During the Great Rebellion of
the South: Illustrated with Thirty-Four Portraits.* (Providence: S.S. Rider
& Brother, 1867) 415-417. Muster Rolls and Descriptive Book of Battery
G, First Rhode Island Light Artillery, Rhode Island State Archives,
Providence, RI.
[3] Walter F. Beyer and Oscar F. Keydel, *Deeds of Valor: How America's
Heroes won the Medal of Honor.* (Detroit: Perrien-Keydel Co., 1901),
515-516.

I spent most of my spare time in 2007 and 2008 when I was a National Park Ranger at Harpers Ferry researching the book. My research trips took me to every battlefield that Battery G fought on in Virginia, West Virginia, Maryland, and Pennsylvania. I was blessed to have the National Archives literally in my backyard and made many research trips there, as well as to the United States Army Military History Institute at Carlisle Barracks, Pennsylvania. During one research trip, I visited Pamplin Historical Park outside Petersburg, Virginia. The park contains a large Civil War museum, as well as the remains of the entrenchments Battery G attacked on April 2, 1865. While touring the museum, I saw a beautiful light artillery bugler's coat, ornately trimmed in gold and red lace. I could not help but notice the neat little hole in the center of the coat's chest, the fatal bullet hole that had struck down the owner of the coat. Reading the sign next to the coat, I was flabbergasted to discover it was owned by a member of Battery G, Bugler William Henry Lewis of Providence.[4]

I promptly found the park historian who told me about the coat, and how it came into the collection. As if almost in passing, he said that Lewis' letters were at the Connecticut State Library in Hartford. I knew that I had to get them as soon as possible. A few phone calls and a week later, I had copies of Lewis' letters written to his mother Jane. The letters, which covered the period from Chancellorsville through Lewis' death at Cedar Creek, provided a wealth of information about Battery G, as well as the campaigns the unit took part in. I readily incorporated the Lewis letters into my book on Battery G, but have long felt they deserved to be published on their own. The majority of the letters concern the battles Lewis fought in, the camp life, and his concerns for his mother and brothers. While these letters are interesting, it is the final two letters in the collection that I feel are most important for the modern reader. The letters written to Jane Lewis after the death

---

[4] The coat of Bugler William Henry Lewis can be seen on page 228 of Don Troiani, Earl J. Coates, and Michael J. McAfee, *Don Troiani's Regiments & Uniforms of the Civil War.* (Mechanicsburg, PA: Stackpole Books, 2002)

of her son tell a poignant and oftentimes forgotten aspect of Civil War combat, those the soldiers left behind.

William Henry Lewis was born in New York in 1845. He was the son of William B. Lewis, a mason born in Rhode Island in 1822, and Jane B. Lewis, a native of Scotland. William had three brothers as well. Jane and William B. Lewis had been married in June 1842 in Providence. According to the 1850 census, the Lewis family lived in the Sixth Ward of Providence, together with other laborers, immigrants, and professionals.[5]

William's childhood was not a pleasant one. In September 1859, Jane filed for divorce in the Supreme Court of Rhode Island, claiming that William B. "has been guilty of continued + habitual drunkenness, and although able so to do hath neglected to provide her and her infant children with necessaries for their subsistence, and had treated her and her children with great cruelty and has been guilty of gross misbehavior + indecency to the petitioner." Furthermore, Jane wanted to "have the custody, care, and guardianship of the children." The court granted the petition, and ordered the divorce. Furthermore, they ordered William B. to be "restrained from intimidating with the said children or their earnings in any manner whatever." Jane maintained her married name of Lewis. William Henry meanwhile obtained employment in in the jewelry industry to support his mother; he continued to attend school and listed his occupation as a "student" when he joined the service. Divorced from her husband, her two sons Theodore and William provided Jane with her only support.[6]

Although from his surviving letters, it appears that William B. and William H. had an estranged relationship, remarkably the father and son pair went together to the Benefit Street Arsenal on November 5, 1861. Here both men enlisted in

---

[5] 1850 U.S. Census, County of Providence, City of Providence, Ward 6, National Archives, Washington, DC. Jane B. Lewis, Divorce Petition, William H. Lewis Pension File, National Archives.

[6] Affidavits of Elizabeth B. Seymour and Theodore S. Seymour, Lewis Pension File. Affidavit of Henry C. Seamans and Frank B. Baker, December 28, 1864, Lewis Pension File. Battery G Descriptive Book.

Battery G, First Rhode Island Light Artillery. William Henry, at age sixteen, was appointed a corporal in the organization. Several other boyhood friends also joined up, including Henry C. Seamans, a cigar maker who considered himself a "brother" of William Henry.[7]

Battery G was a unique organization. It included a very large contingent of men from South County, another section of men from western Rhode Island towns such as Scituate and Coventry, a contingent of native born Yankees from Providence, together with newly arrived Irish and German immigrants; together they all seamlessly blended to work together to man the six guns of the battery. Battery G left Rhode Island on December 2, 1861. Under the command of nineteen-year-old Captain Charles Owen, the battery was assigned to the Second Corps of the Army of the Potomac. They moved to the Peninsula in April 1862 and were engaged at Yorktown and Fair Oaks. William H. Lewis had enlisted as a non-commissioned officer and was supposed to set the example for the men under his command. During the Battle of Fair Oaks, Lewis, together with some of the men ran away from their guns as the Confederates closed in. On June 9, 1862 Captain Owen stripped Lewis and two sergeants of their stripes, writing. "Men who are qualified for the positions of sergts and corpls are wanted and not those who when danger or a little hard work is ahead deliberately stop and refuse to try." [8]

Although demoted from his position as a non-commissioned officer, Lewis apparently had some musical ability and was given the position of bugler, one of two in the battery. After his stripes were removed, Lewis sent them back home to his

---

[7] *Revised Register of Rhode Island Volunteers: Volume II.* (Providence: E.L. Freeman, 1893), 918: 922. See the letters of William H. Lewis at the Connecticut State Library for more information on his relationship with William B. especially see May 21, 1863, June 6, 1863, and June 22, 1863.
[8] General Orders #8, Battery G, First Rhode Island Light Artillery Orderly Book, First Rhode Island Light Artillery Papers, National Archives.

mother in Providence, hoping to earn them again in combat.[9] After Fair Oaks, Battery G spent a miserable month garrisoning a series of fortifications along the Chickahominy River; scores of men came down with typhoid and dysentery. In late June, the Confederates counterattacked and the battery fought in the Seven Days Battles. In September 1862, Battery G was heavily engaged at Antietam, fighting along Dunker Church Ridge and near the Bloody Lane. Further combat came in December at Fredericksburg.

1863 brought a new year and a change for William Henry Lewis. His father was discharged for disability on February 16, 1863 and returned to Providence. In addition, Captain Owen resigned shortly after Fredericksburg. He was replaced by Horace Bloodgood, who resigned a few months later. On May 2, 1863, shortly before the Battle of Chancellorsville, Captain George W. Adams arrived to take command. A native of Providence, a pre-war member of the Providence Marine Corps of Artillery, merchant, and decorated combat veteran, Adams had seen nearly two years of service with Battery B. He earned the respect of the men under his command, and led the battery for the rest of the war; in time Battery G was simply known as "Adams' Battery."[10]

On May 3, 1863 the battery was heavily engaged at Mayre's Heights as part of the Chancellorsville Campaign. The command was sent out early to distract the Confederates as Union forces formed up to storm the hill. In the engagement, Bugler Lewis distinguished himself under fire; after his horse was killed, he joined a gun crew and worked on a cannon during the rest of the battle. Although they lost heavily, seven dead and twenty wounded, the Union forces managed to take the hill. With the death of Bugler Thomas F. Mars in the action, Lewis became chief bugler of the battery, and also acted as a courier and aide for Captain Adams. After the battle, William's father happened to be

---

[9] William H. Lewis to Jane B. Lewis, August 8, 1864, Connecticut State Library.
[10] For more information on Captain George W. Adams, refer to *In Memoriam: George William Adams*. (Providence: NP, 1883), copy at Providence Public Library and author's collection.

in camp bringing packages to the men in Battery G from. He was given the task of bringing the body of Second Lieutenant Benjamin E. Kelley, whom Lewis called "one of our best lieuts," back to Providence. The elder Lewis performed the duty and wrote a detailed letter to the *Providence Journal* informing the people of Rhode Island about the actions of Battery G in the battle. He wrote of his son's bravery and gave a list of casualties. Bugler Lewis was mortified to read that his father called himself Lieutenant Lewis in the article, when he was in fact a discharged private. William B. Lewis had promised to make another trip to bring items to the men in Battery G, but he never did, prompting William Henry to write to his mother that his father was "up to his old ways." Battery G was present, but not engaged at Gettysburg, although they did fight in a rear-guard action on July 5 near Fairfield, Pennsylvania. In November 1863, the command fought at Mine Run.[11]

Battery G began the spring of 1864 as part of the Sixth Corps of the Army of the Potomac. They took part in the actions at the Wilderness, Spotsylvania Court House, Cold Harbor, and Petersburg. In July 1864, the battery was sent to the Shenandoah Valley after a surprise Confederate raid on Washington, DC. Battery G distinguished itself at Cool Spring on July 18, providing pinpoint suppressing fire to support Union forces attacking a Confederate position. In September, the battery fought well at Opequon and Fisher's Hill. After so much marching, campaigning, and combat up and down the Shenandoah Valley, the army rested along the banks of Cedar Creek, south of Middletown, Virginia. That rest was disturbed in the early hours of October 19, when the Confederates attacked. In the ensuing battle, Bugler William Henry Lewis made the ultimate sacrifice, giving his life to save one of the cannon of Battery G from being captured.[12]

---

[11] *Providence Journal,* May 8, 1863. William H. Lewis to Jane B. Lewis, May 21, 1863 and June 22, 1863, Connecticut State Library.

[12] This is a thumbnail sketch of Battery G that is extracted from Robert Grandchamp, *The Boys of Adams' Battery G: The Civil War through the Eyes of a Union Light Artillery Unit.* (Jefferson, NC: McFarland Publishing, 2009)

The letters here are transcribed directly from the originals contained within the Lewis Family Papers at the Connecticut State Library, which has graciously extended permission to publish the letters and images contained within this article.

Letter I. Henry Chase Seamans was a private in Battery G and was Lewis' best friend in the service. Bugler Lewis died of his wounds on October 21, 1864 at a field hospital outside of Middletown, Virginia. Private Seamans was especially pained by the death of Lewis, whom he considered his brother. His older biological brother, Frank Seamans had died in Providence on October 11, 1863 of illness contracted in the service, three months after returning home from a nine-month enlistment in Company D, Eleventh Rhode Island Volunteers. Seamans wrote a hasty letter to Jane Lewis in pencil to inform her that her son had died.

Camp near Middletown Virginia Oct 21st

Mrs. Lewis

With regret I am called to inform you of son William Lewis. He died this morning at half past ten from the effects of his wounds, he was wounded on the 19th. The ball passed through his left side and came out of his right side just below the short rib.[13] I and Edwin Henshaw[14] & a man named Braman[15] dug his grave &

---

[13] Obviously, Lewis was not buried wearing the coat he was shot in, as it is now on display at the Pamplin Park Museum near Petersburg, Virginia.
[14] Private Edwin B. Henshaw was an eighteen-year-old clerk from Providence who transferred to Battery G from Company D, Second Rhode Island Volunteers on December 5, 1863. He was mustered out at Middletown, Virginia on October 31, 1864 and returned to Rhode Island. *Revised Register, Volume II,* 915. Battery G Descriptive Book.
[15] Marcus L. Braman enlisted in Battery G on June 20, 1863; he was listed as a twenty-two-year-old shoemaker who resided in Providence. He was mustered out on June 24, 1865. He died August 26, 1874 and is buried at Old Union Center Cemetery, Union, Connecticut. *Revised Register: Volume II,* 909. Battery G, Descriptive Book. http://www.findagrave.com/cgibin/fg.cgi?page=gr&GSln=braman&GSfn

buried him. He is buried in a cemetery belonging to the town above. I & Frank Baker[16] stayed there after we buried him and fixed his grave in as good shape as if he were buried at home. Your son was loved by all who new him, at the time he was wounded he jumped from the horse he was riding and sprang on to the horses that were harnessed to our gun and by so doing he saved the gun from being captured.

All the men that are left out of our Battery feel deeply with you and Mrs. Lewis no heart can tell how bad I feel, the last words he said to me was these tell my Dear Mother if my would should prove to be fatal that I died an honor to my Mother and my Country. He died happy and said he was willing to go to his God for he said I die a Christian. Billy had one hundred I think 60 dollars due him and you can get all of his Government Bounty by seeing Major Monroe[17] or Paymaster Knight.[18] I would advise you to see them as soon as possible on account of his father for if he

---

=marcus&GSmn=l&GSbyrel=all&GSdyrel=all&GSob=n&GRid=96902 401&df=all&

[16] Frank B. Baker was an eighteen-year-old student and a resident of Apponaug, in Warwick when he enlisted on March 11, 1862. He was mustered out March 11, 1865. *Revised Register,* 908. Battery G, Descriptive Book.

[17] Lieutenant Colonel John Albert Monroe of Providence was born in 1836. A student at Brown University when the war broke out, Monroe was a member of the Providence Marine Corps of Artillery. He enlisted as a lieutenant in Battery A, and quickly was promoted to captain of Battery D. Monroe earned praise for his heroism at Second Manassas and Antietam. After these battles he was promoted to major and lieutenant colonel of the First Rhode Island Light Artillery. He commanded an artillery camp of instruction in Washington, DC, served as an artillery brigade commander, and was mustered out in the fall of 1864. He returned to Providence, and became a civil engineer. Highly active in veterans' affairs, Monroe died in 1891. *Bartlett,* Memoirs of Rhode Island Officers, *405-407*

[18] Jabez Comstock Knight, 1815-1900, was the paymaster general of the Rhode Island Militia. He was mayor of Providence during the Civil War, encouraging enlistments and industry to support the Union. Welcome Greene Arnold, *The Providence Plantations for 250 Years.* (Providence: J.A. & R.A. R.A. Reid, 1886), 104-105.

heard of it, I think he will try to get the money It was ~~Billys~~ Williams request that his mother should have all of his money & all of his pay that are there in the battery. I will send to you by Edwin Henshaw he will be at home in less than 2 weeks as his time is out in seven days.

I have written you all about your son that I can think of at present. I feel deeply with you all and I know that Billy is happy now for he was a good Christian. This sad letter is from me who will ever be willing to help comfort you.

From C. Seamans.[19]

Letter II. A month after the battle, as Battery G returned to Washington, DC to consolidate with Battery C, First Rhode Island Light Artillery, obtain new horses and guns, and recuperate from the hard-fought campaign in the Shenandoah Valley, Henry Seamans had time to write another letter to Jane Lewis.

Camp Russell Va November 30, 64

Mrs. Lewis.

Your long looked for letter reached me this morning. I was and have been anxious to hear from you. It seems so lonsome without Billy to talk with. We were as you say the same as Brothers together. He was a good soldier and a brave one and he will never be forgotten in our Battery. Every day there is some one talking about him. Well it was *Gods* will that he should die and if

---

[19] Henry Chase Seamans enlisted from Providence into Battery G on December 17, 1861; he gave his occupation as a cigar maker and stated he was sixteen-years old. He reenlisted as a veteran volunteer in 1863. Seamans was mustered out on June 24, 1865. He died in Providence on September 3, 1886, and is buried at North Burial Ground. Battery G, Descriptive Book.
http://www.findagrave.com/cgibin/fg.cgi?page=gr&GSln=seamans&GSfn=henry+&GSmn=c&GSbyrel=all&GSdyrel=all&GSob=n&GRid=33275223&df=all&

186

we are good on this earth we shall surely meet him in Heaven for Billy was a good Christian. You ask me how much money he had coming to him. He had three hundred and fifty dollars coming to him from the Government acct was his bounty money & he had three months pay coming to him and the whole amount that is due him as near as I think is between three hundred & ninety dollars & four hundred dollars.[20] I went to my Captain[21] and asked him about his clothing, and he said they would have to be sent some in a military form what he meant by that I cant make out. You say that you have not been able to do anything since your sons death. Don't I pray you feel to bad about it we have all die some time. God would not took your son from this wicked world if he had not thought best Billy is far more happier ware he is now than he would be in this world and at Gods appointed time we will all see him never to part again. Wont that be a joyous meeting ware war or suffering never comes. I feel so happy to think he was buried so good but it was a hard task for me. You say if you could get his money, you would get his body. His body is not in our lines at present since my last letter to you the army has fallen back about six miles, so you see it would be impossible to get to it at present and I think it would only be a bill of expense to you. If you should come out to get him for his is buried just as well as if he were at home and with as respect. His grave is besides one that has been there for nearly fifty years. I don't see what delayed my first letter so long. I hope this letter will reach you in due season and also find you all in good health and spirits. Tell Eddie I will write to him soon, my respects to all of you. Tell George & Theodore[22] I should like to hear from them by mail. There is no news at present. The Army is settled for the winter and the Soldiers are building

---

[20] In December 1863, William Henry Lewis reenlisted as a veteran volunteer and received a thirty-five-day furlough home, as well as a substantial bounty to serve another enlistment. It was during this furlough back to Providence, accompanied by Seamans, that the only known images of Lewis were taken. William H. Lewis, Service File, National Archives. William H. Lewis, photographs, William H. Lewis Papers, Connecticut State Library.

[21] Captain George W. Adams of Providence commanded Battery G. *Providence Journal,* October 17, 1883.

[22] The sons of Jane B. and William B. Lewis.

log houses. I have got my hut finished myself and Frank Baker live together and we are comfortable. We are comfortable as can be, we got plenty to eat and plenty to wear at present. The weather is warm, but we have has some very cold weather and some snow. Well I will close by saying that I shall ever be glad to have you write to me. I will close by subscribing myself your friend.

Henry C. Seamans

Please Direct
Battery "G" R I L A
Sixth Corps
Army of the Shenandoah
Washington D.C.

Do I direct my letters right

H.C.S.

Letter III. Memorial poetry was typically written by the family of Civil War soldiers who died in the service as a means to remember their service. Some of these poems were printed in local newspapers, while broadsides were made of others for distribution to family and friends. This poem, memorializing William H. Lewis was written by Irene P. Williams.

William H. Lewis Buglar
Wounded Oct. 19 Died the 21st
Aged 19 years.

But Jesus has called the loved one away,
A son, has gone to rest:
Far from this earth where death holds away
He dwells among the blest.

I speak of one who left this state
When his country's voice come;
How sad, and mournful was his fate

188

He died far, far, from home.

While nobly fighting on the field,
A deadly missile from the foe
Pierced through his sides, there was nothing to shield
The tiding to his home brought woe.

No Mothers smile from day to day,
Brightened the weary hour;
In vain was human skill to stay
Deaths unrelenting power.

When far from home and those he loved
What must his thoughts have been,
Perchance with fancys eyes he roved
In the streets at home again.

Lord Jesus called him hence from earth
Then wherefore will ye mourn;
His souls to God who gave it birth
Has gone to an eternal home.

Fond Mother, look beyond the grave
Your sons is now in heaven,
Eternal life he there will have
By God's own hand tis given.

Rest loved one rest, though here on earth
Mother, and brothers, mourn thy loss
From scenes of war you're gone we trust,
Where gold is never mixes with dross

Nov. 19th 1864, Providence
Irene P. Williams.

Despite the hard work that Henry Seamans and his comrades performed to give William H. Lewis a proper burial spot, he would not rest in the town cemetery in Middletown, Virginia forever. Heeding Seamans' letter, Jane Lewis never returned her son's body to Providence. Beginning in 1865, the Federal government began to remove the remains of Union soldiers who died in the northern Shenandoah Valley to the new Winchester National Cemetery, which was dedicated on April 8, 1866. Here in Grave 3589, William Henry Lewis rests near four other Battery G soldiers who died in the early morning fight for the guns at Cedar Creek. After the war, many other states, including Vermont, Connecticut, Massachusetts, and New Hampshire dedicated monuments at Winchester National Cemetery to commemorate the valor of their sons who fought in the Shenandoah Valley. A monument was never dedicated to the Rhode Islanders who fought and died in the Shenandoah.[23]

Following Seamans' advice, Jane Lewis began the process of obtaining a mother's pension. She filed on November 22, 1864 in Providence, claiming she had been divorced since 1859. Lewis attested, "She declares that her said son, upon whom she was wholly or in part dependent for support, having left no widow or minor children under sixteen years." She claimed that William had supported her after the divorce, and had sent the majority of his pay back to Providence to support his mother and brothers. Two neighbors supported these facts.[24]

In addition to the support of her neighbors, Jane turned to the two men who knew her son the most and could attest best to the fact that William Henry supported his mother during his Civil War service:

> State of Rhode Island
> City and County of Providence
>
> On the 28th day of December 1865 personally appeared before me a Public Notary within + for the County and State aforesaid Frank B. Baker residency of No. 26 "A"

---

[23] National Cemetery Administration, Winchester National Cemetery, accessed October 29, 2016,
http://www.cem.va.gov/CEM/cems/nchp/winchester.asp
[24] Jane B. Lewis, Declaration for Mother's Pension, November 22, 1864, Lewis Pension File. Seymour Affidavits, Lewis Pension File.

Street in this city of Providence and Henry C. Seamans of No. 148 Carpenter Street in said City persons whom I certify to be respectable and entitled to credit who being by me duly sword according to law say that they well knew Jane B. Lewis of said city applicant for pension. That they have known her for the past five years that she is the widow of William B. Lewis who is in such a situation that she cannot enforce her legal claim upon him for subsistence by reason of having divorced from him, and the Mother of William Henry Lewis who entered the military service of the United States and died in such service. That they well knew said William Henry Lewis in his life time that he left no wife or child surviving him and that he contributed to the support of his said mother out of his earnings. That he was employed in the jewelry manufacturing business a the weekly wages of five dollars before entering the military service aforesaid and that said Wm. Henry Lewis has repeatedly told said deponents that he gave all up his said wages to his mother. That said William after he entered the military service aforesaid *repeatedly* sent his said mother portions of his pay both by *express* and also through the state *allotment commissioner*. That we were members of the same Battery "G" 1st Regt R.I. Light Artillery Vols and were quite intimate with the said William Henry Lewis and we have seen letters which he received from his said Mother in which she acknowledged the receipt of the money which the said William sent to her and he repeatedly told us while in the military service aforesaid that he helped support his Mother. Also that the said Jane B. Lewis had *no property* and her present means of support is keeping boarders. That deponents as aforesaid have no interest in the prosecution of this claim.

Frank B. Baker

Henry C. Seamans[25]

Unlike many other soldiers, widows, orphans, and mothers, Jane Lewis did not have relatively long to wait in obtaining her first pension check. She began to be paid eight dollars per month, beginning on February 9, 1866, with back pay to October 22, 1864, the day after William died. In 1871, the name "W.H. Lewis" was inscribed on the Soldiers and Sailors Monument in Providence, listing the young man as an official Civil War casualty from Rhode Island. Jane's divorced husband, William B. Lewis died in Cranston on December 7, 1882. He was buried in the Grand Army of the Republic Lot in North Burial Ground in Providence. By the time she died in Providence on March 18, 1908, Jane was receiving twelve dollars per month. It was small compensation in memory of her beloved son William who died forty-two years earlier saving a gun from capture at Cedar Creek.[26]

---

[25] Baker and Seamans Affidavit, Lewis Service File.
[26] *Proceedings at the Dedication of the Soldiers and Sailors Monument in Providence, To which is Appended a list of the Deceased Soldiers and Sailors whose Names are Sculptured upon the Monument.* (Providence: A. Crawford Greene, 1871), 62. Burial Records of Prescott Post #1, Grand Army of the Republic Papers, Rhode Island Historical Society. Jane B. Lewis Pension Certificate and Pension Drop Certificate in Lewis Pension File.

Chapter Fourteen:

"Scarce a man but lost a friend or relative:"

A letter from the Battle of Fredericksburg

Since I was fifteen years old, I have studied the small, but I feel, important role that the Seventh Rhode Island Volunteers, my great-great-great uncle's regiment, played in the Civil War. This research has brought me to literally every town hall, cemetery, library, and archive in Rhode Island, and many more throughout the country. In addition, I have followed the regiment's path from the streets of Fredericksburg, to the swamps of Mississippi, across Ohio and Kentucky, to the killing fields of central Virginia. Over the course of nearly half my life studying the Seventh, one date has always been omnipresent: December 13, 1862, the Battle of Fredericksburg.

Over the course of five hours on that bloody, muddy, cold, and terrible Saturday, 570 Rhode Islanders demonstrated what they were capable of under the command of Colonel Zenas Randall Bliss. Marching into a hailstorm of artillery and musket fire, the Seventh, against all odds, kept on going, until they could go no further without being destroyed. The regiment made it to within seventy-five yards of their objective. Although the Seventh, in the remaining two and a half years of its Civil War service would suffer terribly due to tropical diseases in the swamps of Mississippi, and during forty days of non-stop combat in the spring of 1864, Fredericksburg was the defining moment in the regiment's history. Although devastated by severe losses, the battle molded the Seventh into a veteran combat outfit to be depended upon again and again. Furthermore, the day was celebrated by the veterans of the Seventh from 1873 until 1926 as they choose it as the day to hold their annual reunions on.[1]

Arguably one of the best, if somewhat under used resources to study the Civil War and Rhode Island is from period newspapers. Unlike many other states, few Civil War era newspapers from Rhode Island are digitized. The researcher is still required to use the old fashion microfilm system. For those who do, papers such as *The Woonsocket Patriot, Narragansett Times, Pawtucket Gazette,* and even the venerable daily *Providence Journal,* provide a wealth of period accounts regarding the Civil War. With no censorship, newspapers would print verbatim from soldier's letters sent from the front, providing one of the best accounts of the period. Although it is tedious, and strains the eyes, this material is very rewarding for the researcher.

The *Narragansett Weekly* is one such newspaper. First published as a weekly in 1855, the paper is still published today as *The Westerly Sun.* During the Civil War period, the *Narragansett Weekly* published dozens of accounts relating to the Civil War soldiers from south-west Rhode Island and nearby Stonington, Connecticut. It is one of the primary sources that I have drawn from time and again to tell the story of the men of Company A of the Seventh Rhode Island Volunteers.

Raised largely from the mill workers, farmers, and laborers of Charlestown, Richmond, Hopkinton, and Westerly in July and early August 1862, Company A was one of ten that composed the Seventh Rhode Island. The unit was initially commanded by Captain Lewis Leavens, a mill overseer from the village of Canonchet in central Hopkinton. Together with the Rev. Joseph Morton, a Seventh Day Baptist minister, and the then principal of the Hopkinton Academy in Ashaway, the two men

---

[1] For a complete history of the Seventh refer to Robert Grandchamp, *The Seventh Rhode Island Infantry in the Civil War.* (Jefferson, NC: McFarland, 2008) Seventh Rhode Island Veterans Association, Books and Papers, author's collection.

raised the fifty Hopkinton soldiers who composed the bulk of the company. After the town council promised a bounty of three hundred dollars, the company was filled within three days. Although leaders in the community, both men experienced only the very briefest of the horrors of war.[2]

Immediately after arriving in Washington in September of 1862, a typhoid outbreak erupted in Company A, killing half-dozen men from south-west Rhode Island, and left dozens sick in the hospital. The Rev. Lieutenant Morton had enough of war, and went back to his pulpit in Ashaway in early December. Leavens stayed with the regiment for another month, leading the company into action at Fredericksburg where he received a slight wound. For many of the Seventh's officers, the battle, the worst of the war for Rhode Island troops must have been terrifying. Half of the original officers that the Seventh left Rhode Island with had resigned their commissions within six months of leaving the state; Leavens was among those who went home.[3]

News of the battle of Fredericksburg, and the terrible losses suffered by the Seventh began to arrive via telegraph several days after the battle. By Christmas of 1862, there was hardly anyone in the state who did not know of a friend, neighbor, or relative who had been killed or wounded in the battle; eighty Rhode Islanders died and over 300 more were wounded.[4]

---

[2] *Narragansett Weekly,* August 7, 1862 and August 21, 1862. William P. Hopkins, *The Seventh Regiment of Rhode Island Volunteers in the Civil War.* (Providence: Snow and Farnum, 1903), 349-350: 368-370.
[3] Kris VanDenBossche , ed. *"Pleas Excuse All Bad Writing:" A Documentary History of Rhode Island during the Civil War Era.* (PeaceDale: Rhode Island Historical Document Transcription Project, 1993), 59-71.
[4] *Providence Journal,* December 15-30, 1862. *Narragansett Times,* December 19, 1862. Elisha Hunt Rhodes, *All for the Union: The Civil War Diary and Letters of Elisha Hunt Rhodes.* Edited by Robert Hunt Rhodes. (Woonsocket: Andrew Mowbray, 1985), 90-93. Fredericksburg represented the largest gathering of Rhode Island troops during the war, and as such, the casualties were significantly higher than any other engagement. The bulk of the losses were from the Seventh and Twelfth Rhode Island infantry regiments that took part in the main assault against

Tryphena Cundall of Ashaway had a son, Isaac, who served in the ranks of Company A; fortunately, he was still sick in the hospital with typhoid during the engagement, and missed the slaughter. Her diary entry for December 19, 1862 is one of the most poignant written about the reaction in Rhode Island to the losses the Seventh Rhode Island suffered at Fredericksburg:

> The army have had a battle but were driven and it is reported that our loss is 13,000 killed, wounded and missing. What a multitude to be swept off at once, many thousand wounded. Oh the anguish the pain with no wife or mother or sister to sooth or nurse or even to give a cup of water. My heart aches for the loves ones. Many very many have fallen to rise no more by to be huddled into the grave of a battlefield. Many more will die of wounds received on the 13th of Dec 1862 at Fredericksburg Virginia and many more will linger out a life maimed, crippled, and suffering. What can I write, how can I express my feelings, it is in vain to try.[5]

Company A went into the battle with roughly fifty officers and men. Three soldiers were killed in action, twenty-one were wounded, and one was captured. Although heavy, this pales in comparison to the losses in South Kingstown's Company G, which lost twelve dead and fourteen wounded.[6]

To relieve the fears of the parents, relatives, and neighbors of the men in Company A, Captain Leavens wrote a very descriptive letter to the *Narragansett Weekly,* describing what happened to the regiment at Fredericksburg, paying particular attention to the role of Company A in the battle. Leavens account

---

Marye's Heights. Also present was the Second and Fourth Rhode Island Infantry, the First Rhode Island Cavalry, and Batteries A, B, C, D, E, and G of the First Rhode Island Light Artillery.

[5] *Pleas Excuse,* 70-71.

[6] Seventh Rhode Island Casualty Returns, Battle of Fredericksburg, James Harris Papers, R.I. Historical Society. Regimental Returns, author's collection and Rhode Island State Archives, Providence, RI.

is one of the best of the dozens I have read about the Seventh
Rhode Island's charge. His comment "Scarce a man but lost a
friend or relative," remains a very powerful statement to the
unimaginable losses the Seventh suffered that terrible day. This
letter was printed in the December 25, 1862 edition of the
Narragansett Weekly.

Co. A, 7th R.I.V.

Camp Opposite Fredericksburg, Va., Dec. 17, 1862

To the Editor of the Narragansett Weekly,

As many, if not all of your readers feel an interest in the
welfare of my company (A) of the 7th Regiment R.I.V., I beg
permission to fill a small space of your columns, hoping and
trusting, that though my statements be brief, yet they may appease
the anxieties of those of your readers who have friends with me
that were engaged in the great and unequaled battle of
Fredericksburg.

At three o'clock on Thursday morning, we were awakened
from our slumbers by the booming of heavy cannon in the
direction of the city. Immediately after, the "long roll" was beaten
by our drum corps, and the *"bloody Seventh"* fell into line, and
marched to the scene of action. All day long we lay behind our
entrenchments, while from the mouths of a hundred batteries sped
the iron missiles of death, dealing destruction and ruin in their
murderous course. But with the close of the day came a cessation
of the most tremendous artillery duel ever yet recorded in the
annals of warfare, and we returned to our quarters, disappointed
that we were not permitted to get sights at the miserable "gray
backs."

Our disappointment, however, was not of long duration;
for at early dawn on Friday morning, we were again ordered into
line, and told by our gallant Colonel,[7] that we were to cross the

---

[7] Colonel Zenas Randall Bliss of Johnston, 1835-1900, was the
commander of the Seventh. An 1854 graduate of West Point, he had
served six years on the Texas frontier in the U.S. Army before being

river on the pontoon bridges, which had been completed during the night. With a quick step and anxious expectations, we followed our Colonel across the river and into Fredericksburg, where we remained in the street near the river until Saturday morning at sunrise, when we formed in line, and in a few brief words our Colonel told us we were to take part in the battle of the day.

Soon after eight o'clock, the first range of batteries south and west of Fredericksburg, occupied by the Confederates, opened on our division. How many guns were in position to rake and decimate our ranks, it is impossible to day; but they were well directed, quickly worked, and told severely upon us. Our batteries on the north side of the Rappahannock replied promptly, and the shells shrieked over the city, across the intervening plain, and into their entrenchments. This continued for about two hours, making the very earth to shake, and tremble. The old soldiers, themselves veterans of nine battles called it terrific. While this was going on, Gen. Meagher formed his "Irish Brigade," marched up the streets exposed to a murderous fire, deployed to the right, and attacked the first line of rifle pits.

Firm, cool, and solid as though each regiment was made of steel, they charged, closely followed by Gen. Nagle's Brigade, our regiment forming a part.[8] Better fighting was never witnessed on the Peninsula, at Antietam, or even in the war of the Crimea. Column after column went down to rise no more. But fresh

---

captured at the start of the Civil War. He was appointed to command the Seventh in the summer of 1862. Beloved by his men, he was awarded the Medal of Honor for his heroism at Fredericksburg. After the battle, Bliss commanded a brigade or separate garrison for the rest of the war. He stayed in the Army after the Civil War and was eventually promoted to major general before retiring in 1897. He is buried at Arlington National Cemetery. Hopkins, *Seventh Rhode Island,* 311-314.

[8] Brigadier General James Nagle of Pennsylvania commanded the First Brigade, Second Division, Ninth Corps consisting of the Sixth and Ninth New Hampshire, Seventh and Twelfth Rhode Island, Second Maryland, and Forty-Eighth Pennsylvania. Francis A. O'Reilly, *The Fredericksburg Campaign: Winter War on the Rappahannock.* (Baton Rouge: Louisiana State University Press, 2003), 329-348.

supports came up with Gen Ferraro,[9] and after three hours of continued hard fighting, in which our regiment received the blunt of the enemy's fire, the heights were carried.[10]

No sooner was this accomplished, than the rebels opened from another line off fortifications, higher up toward the crest of the hills, that overlooked and commanded the city. Here again was another scene of greater carnage. Grape and canister were thrown among us with awful effect, and it soon became evident that this second line could not be carried without the aid of a field battery then lying across the plain, one-fourth of a mile to the rear, and sheltered in the streets of the city.[11]

Some one must go for the battery. Col. Bliss called John P. Jones,[12] who had shown great bravery during the action to perform the hazardous duty of carrying the order to the Captain of the battery; but Jones refused, and Sergeant Peleg E. Peckham was then ordered to carry out the order, for the execution of which he deserved much credit.[13] Through the thickest of the fight, exposed

---

[9] Brigadier General Edward Ferraro of New York commanded the Second Brigade, Second Division, Ninth Corps composed of the Fifty-First New York, Fifty-First Pennsylvania, Twenty-First and Thirty-Fifth Massachusetts, and the Eleventh New Hampshire. O'Reilly, *Fredericksburg,* 329-348.

[10] Leavens is wrong in his account. While Union troops managed to break through the Confederate line to the south of the Seventh's position at a place called Prospect Hill, no Union troops broke through at the infamous stone wall at the base of Marye's Heights. Reilly, *Fredericksburg,* 127-145.

[11] Leavens references Battery C, Fourth United States Artillery under the command of Lieutenant Evan Thomas. The battery, part of the Second Corps, provided covering fire for the charge of the Second Division, Ninth Corps. Reilly, *Fredericksburg,* 329.

[12] Private John P. Jones of Providence was a thirty-two-year-old married clerk when he enlisted on July 2, 1862. He survived the war unscathed and was mustered out on June 9, 1862. Company A, Seventh Rhode Island Volunteers, Descriptive Book, Rhode Island State Archives.

[13] A carpenter from Charlestown, Peleg Edwin Peckham was promoted to second lieutenant for his actions. He was eventually promoted to captain of Company A, and earned a brevet majority for heroism at Spotsylvania

to a murderous fire from the enemy, being for the whole distance in full view of their sharpshooters, he went and performed his duty, bringing out the battery, which took position on our right, in time to turn the flank of the enemy, and enabled us to hold our position until 8 o'clock when we were relieved by the 3d division of our corps, having been exposed to the rebel batteries and sharpshooters for eight hours.

Both our officers and men behaved admirably, and won merited praise from our Generals.[14] We passed the night on our arms in the city, but to many it was a sleepless one. Sunday morning dawned upon us, but sorry faces composed our broken and thinned ranks. Scarce a man but had lost a friend or relative; the cries of and moans of the wounded and dying were indescribable. All day, both Sunday and Monday, we lay in the streets of Fredericksburg, and in the evening evacuated the place, satisfied that we had been sadly outgeneraled and "badly whipped." And that the rebels *cannot* be driven from their strongholds back of Fredericksburg in the manner the attempt has just been made.

The loss in our Regiment, in killed, wounded, and missing is one hundred and eighty.[15] I give the names and nature of wounds, as far as I know:

Court House. Peckham was killed in action on April 2, 1865 at Petersburg, VA. See Robert Grandchamp, "The Letters of Major Peleg Edwin Peckham." *Rhode Island Roots,* Vol. 35 No. 1, March 2009, pp. 21-29.

[14] The Seventh's performance in the battle earned the praise of their brigade, division, and corps commanders. See Augustus Woodbury, *Major General Ambrose E. Burnside and the Ninth Army Corps: A Narrative of Campaigns in North Carolina, Maryland, Virginia, Ohio, Kentucky, Mississippi, and Tennessee during the War for the Preservation of the Republic.* (Providence: Sidney S. Rider, 1867), 223-224. Woodbury wrote, "They stood at their posts with the steadiness of veterans, they advanced with the enthusiasm of genuine soldiers, they won the encomium of all who witnessed their valor on this their first day of battle."

[15] Estimates of the Seventh's losses at Fredericksburg have been calculated from a low of 130 to a high of 220, depending on the source.

Capt. Lewis Leavens, slight.
Lieut David R. Kenyon, contusion to leg[16]
Corporal Wm. B. Neff, shot through the leg[17]
Corporal Horace Wells, in left shoulder[18]

Privates

Geo. B. Albro, slightly.[19]

Arguably many of those who suffered minor wounds never went to the hospital, while some men who died even months after the battle from their wounds were not recorded among the dead. Nearly forty men became separated from the unit during the battle, and did not report until the Seventh was back across the river. A *very* careful search of all available service and pension records, muster rolls, and the soldier's letters puts the Seventh's final tally at forty-nine dead, 145 wounded, and three captured, for a total of 197. This is still the highest battlefield loss of any Rhode Island regiment in any battle of any war. Zenas R. Bliss, *The Reminiscences of Major General Zenas R. Bliss, 1854-1876.* Edited by Thomas T. Smith, Jerry D. Thompson, Robert Wooster, and Ben E. Pingenot. (Austin: Texas State Historical Society, 2007), 324-331. Hopkins, *Seventh Rhode Island,* 57-59. Seventh Rhode Island Regimental Returns, Rhode Island State Archives.

[16] David R. Kenyon of Richmond was a twenty-nine-year-old married "manufacturer" who recruited most of the Richmond contingent for Company A. Wounded in the leg at Fredericksburg; he was promoted to captain of Company I, but resigned in March 1863. After the war he continued working in the mill industry, and served in a variety of civic officers; he died in 1897. He is buried in Wood River Cemetery, Richmond. Hopkins, *Seventh Rhode Island,* 349.

[17] Corporal William B. Neff was a twenty-seven-year-old married farmer from Glocester who enlisted August 5, 1862. He was severely wounded in the left thigh at Fredericksburg, and was transferred to the Veterans Reserve Corps on November 30, 1863. Company A Descriptive Book, Rhode Island State Archives.

[18] Corporal Horace Wells, a twenty-one-year-old single farmer from Hopkinton enlisted August 7, 1862. Wounded in the left shoulder at Fredericksburg, he was discharged for disability February 1, 1863. Company A Descriptive Book, Rhode Island State Archives.

[19] Nineteen-year-old George B. Albro of Coventry was a laborer, who enlisted July 24, 1862. Shot in the leg at Fredericksburg, he was sent to

Patrick Burke, slightly.[20]
John B. Clarke, slightly.[21]
Henry Gardner, wrist.[22]
John R. Greene, foot amputated.[23]
Michael Flaherty, in leg.[24]
Richard Weeden, seriously.[25]
Geo. H. Brown, in leg.[26]

---

the hospital, but returned to the regiment, and was mustered out June 9, 1865. He is buried in the Hope Cemetery, Scituate, RI. Company A Descriptive Book, Rhode Island State Archives.

[20] Patrick Burke, a twenty-four-year-old married farmer from Richmond enlisted August 9, 1862. He was shot in the leg at Fredericksburg, and also in the arm May 12, 1864 at Spotsylvania. He was discharged for disability May 26, 1865. Company A Descriptive Book, Rhode Island State Archives.

[21] John Burr Clark was a twenty-eight-year-old married farmer from Richmond. Shot in the back at Fredericksburg, he was sent to a hospital in Baltimore, where he died of his wounds on May 10, 1863. Company A Descriptive Book, Rhode Island State Archives.

[22] Henry C. Gardner, a sixteen-year-old farmer from Hopkinton enlisted August 8, 1862. Shot in the arm at Fredericksburg, he was promoted to corporal, was shot in the hand at Spotsylvania, and sent to the Veterans Reserve Corps on December 17, 1864. Company A Descriptive Book, Rhode Island State Archives.

[23] Twenty-eight-year-old John R. Greene was a married farmer from Hopkinton. His left foot was amputated due to his battle wounds, and he was discharged for disability on February 6, 1863. Company A Descriptive Book, Rhode Island State Archives.

[24] Sergeant Michael Flaherty of Providence was shot in the leg at Fredericksburg, and did not return to the regiment until February 1863. He was later killed in action June 3, 1864 at Bethesda Church, VA. Company A Descriptive Book, Rhode Island State Archives.

[25] An eighteen-year-old laborer from Providence, Weeden was wounded at Fredericksburg, and was sent to Portsmouth Grove Hospital, where he was later discharged. Company A Descriptive Book, Rhode Island State Archives.

[26] Twenty-year-old George Henry Brown was a hatter from Richmond. Wounded at Fredericksburg, he was shot again in the leg at Spotsylvania, and transferred to the Veterans Reserve Corps. He is buried in Pine Grove Cemetery in Hopkinton. Company A Descriptive Book, Rhode Island State Archives.

Horace Slocum, in head.[27]
Charles H. Holdridge, slightly.[28]
Geo. C. Wells, slightly.[29]
Edward Larkin, slightly.[30]
Joel B. Gorton, slightly.[31]
Jedediah Green, supposed killed.[32]

All the above wounded are doing well, except Geo. C. Wells. I have not found him since the battle, but have good authority for saying that he is in some of the hospitals, and has not

---

[27] Horace Slocum, a single twenty-year-old spinner from Richmond was shot in the hand at Fredericksburg. At the North Anna River in May 1864, Slocum was shot in the back. He is buried in Pine Grove Cemetery, Hopkinton. Company A Descriptive Book, Rhode Island State Archives.
[28] An eighteen-year-old wheelwright from Ashaway, Holdridge received a head injury at Fredericksburg, for which he was discharged March 2, 1863. Holdridge was the last survivor of Company A, and died April 10, 1937 at 92. He is buried in Oak Grove Cemetery, Hopkinton. *Westerly Sun,* April 11, 1937. Company A Descriptive Book, Rhode Island State Archives.
[29] A single farmer from Hopkinton, Wells was shot at Fredericksburg, and was discharged for disability at Washington January 12, 1863. Company A Descriptive Book, Rhode Island State Archives.
[30] A twenty-four-year-old married farmer from Richmond, Larkin enlisted August 8, 1862. Shot in the left knee, he returned to the regiment, and was mustered out June 9, 1865. Company A Descriptive Book, Rhode Island State Archives.
[31] Twenty-one-year-old Joel B. Gorton was a farmer from West Greenwich when he enlisted August 12, 1862. He was wounded at Fredericksburg, and died of Yazoo Fever at Camp Nelson, KY on September 11, 1863. He is buried at Camp Nelson National Cemetery, Grave D 1262. Company A Descriptive Book, Rhode Island State Archives.
[32] Forty-two-year-old Jedediah Greene was one of the oldest men in Company A. A married laborer from Hopkinton, he was killed in action at Fredericksburg, and his body was never recovered. Company A Descriptive Book, RISA.

been able to report himself here. I am told by those who saw him, his wound was in the arm.

But I have for this time written perhaps enough to weary the patience of your readers.

Your obedient servant

Lewis Leavens
Capt. Co. A, 7th R.I.V.

Chapter Fifteen:

Lines on the Death of Alfred S. Knight

      The following is a transcription of the poem that was written by Almon Knight, Alfred Sheldon Knight's cousin and discovered by the author in 2001 which led to his lifetime interest in the Seventh Rhode Island Volunteers. The copy preserved in the author's collection was enclosed in a death notice for Almon who died on August 22, 1922. Several stanzas of this poem were used as Alfred's epitaph.

Lines on the Death of
Alfred S. Knight,

Private of Company C, 7th Regiment R.I.V.
Who died in the Regimental Hospital
Falmouth, January 31, 1863.

When last we saw him on his cheek,
The glow of health was bright,
The stamp of manhood on his brown,
And in his eye Hope's light.

He went from us with noble thoughts,
With high and holy aim,
With fond hope whispering in his heart,
That he'd come home again.

Alas! bright hope how vain
Are all thy flattering dreams!
How quickly pales the brightest star
That in thy future dreams!

Far from the home he loved so well
He met an early doom
No mother near to sooth his brow
Or cheer him mid deaths gloom.

No sister's gentle form was there
To hover round his bed,
To pillow with a sister's love
That wildly throbbing head.

Far from his kindred and from all
His fond heart held most dear,-
Oh! was there none in that far land
To shed for him a tear?

Was no one near in that sad hour,
That trembling hand to press;
To give for dear ones far away
Affection's last find kiss?

Oh! yes; methinks, amongst that band
Of soldiers, brave and strong,
That many tears fell for him,
And that they'll morn him long.

O Stricken parents weep no more
Bright the Crown to him that's given:
You'll meet your noble son again
In the bright land of heaven.

Brothers and sisters though he'll join
For here on Earth no more,
United you shall be again
On heavens immortal shore.

No cruel Death can enter there,
In those bright realms above;
No parting tears are ever shed,
But all is peace and love.

Acknowledgements

At the Rhode Island State Archives, Ken Carlson was instrumental in finding many of the smaller government publications.

In Providence, General Richard Valente provided access to the Benefit Street Arsenal and its vast resources while I was working on the book *Rhody Redlegs*. The staffs at the Rhode Island Historical Society, Providence City Hall Archives, Brown University, and the Providence Public Library were equally helpful. My old comrade Caleb Horton, the Providence city archivist shared his research on the soldiers of Providence.

Captain Phil DiMaria of Battery B has been a mentor, friend, and guide for nearly twenty years as I navigated and researched the role of Rhode Island in the Civil War era. Without Phil's assistance and guidance, none of this work would have been possible.

Nina Wright and the staff at the Westerly Public Library always provided access and many photocopies when I visited that wonderful institution, as did Matt Reardon of the New England Civil War Museum in Rockville, Connecticut.

Meredith Dyer Sweet, Shirley Arnold, Rachel Peirce, Midge Frazel, and the many other descendants of Rhode Island's soldiers who shared material about their ancestors with me over the years are to be given a special amount of gratitude. Without their contributions, this book would be much smaller.

At the Varnum Continentals, Patrick Donovan provided access to the collections and listened to my many stories. Colonel Richard Sheryka has always been of great assistance in providing information on the Kentish Guards.

Cherry Fletcher Bamberg of the Rhode Island Genealogical Society is to be commended to guiding my research and writing over the years as I wrote many articles for *Rhode Island Roots*.

Master Sergeant Jim Loffler, the historical section chief of the Rhode Island National Guard is always of great assistance in providing information on the history of Rhode Island soldiers. Russell DeSimone and Christian McBurney were also helpful in this department.

Although many years have passed, the interlibrary loan staff and Marlene Lopes at Rhode Island College Special Collections will always be remembered for their assistance in finding long lost books and articles while I was a student there from 2004-2010.

Many of these sources were found in various repositories throughout Rhode Island and although I may not have remembered names, I do wish to thank these institutions that assisted in this work: Langworthy Public Library, East Providence Historical Society, Foster Preservation Society, Scituate Preservation Society, Newport Historical Society, Pettaquamscutt Historical Society, Richmond Historical Society, Redwood Library, Burrillville Historical and Preservation Society, Glocester Heritage Society, Bristol Historical Society, North Kingstown Public Library, East Greenwich Public Library, Westerly Armory Foundation, Connecticut State Library, Yale University, and the South County Museum.

My mother Patricia Townsend Grandchamp and grandmother, Joyce Knight Townsend nurtured a love of history in me at an early age, took me to battlefields, bought me books, and patiently waited while I waded through research at museums and libraries. For their dedication, I will be forever grateful.

Lastly, I must thank my dear wife Elizabeth. She has the patience of a saint and gladly lives with the Civil War every day.

About the Author

Robert Grandchamp first became interested in Rhode Island's role in the Civil War in 2001, after learning from his grandmother that his third great uncle, Alfred Sheldon Knight had served in the Seventh Rhode Island Volunteers as a private in Company C and died of pneumonia serving in the Civil War. Trips to battlefields, libraries, and archives fueled his interest and he soon began to collect material for a regimental history of the Seventh Rhode Island that was published in 2008 as *The Seventh Rhode Island Infantry in the Civil War.* Among his other works are *Rhody Redlegs, The Boys of Adams' Battery G, Colonel Edward E. Cross, Rhode Island and the Civil War: Voices from the Ocean State,* and *A Connecticut Yankee at War: The Life and Letters of George Lee Gaskell.* Robert earned his M.A. in American history from Rhode Island College, in addition to his B.A. in anthropology and American history from Rhode Island College as well. He is a former National Park Ranger with service at Shenandoah and Harpers Ferry battlefield. For his efforts to honor the soldiers from Rhode Island, Robert has been awarded the Order of Saint Barbara from the Rhode Island National Guard, the Margaret B. Stillwell Prize from the John Russell Bartlett Society at Brown University, as well as letters of commendation from the governor of Rhode Island and mayor of Providence. Among his professional affiliations, he is a longtime member of several historical organizations, including the Rhode Island Genealogical Society. Robert is an analyst with the Federal government and resides with his wife Elizabeth and their children in Jericho Center, Vermont.